CREATIVE IDEAS
FOR
CHRISTMAS
1986

COMPILED AND EDITED BY NANCY JANICE FITZPATRICK

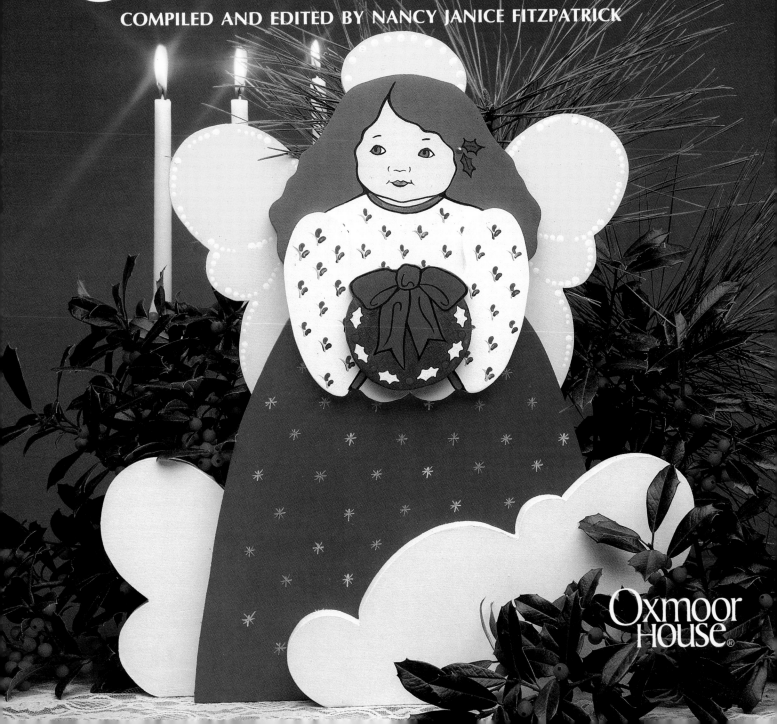

Oxmoor House®

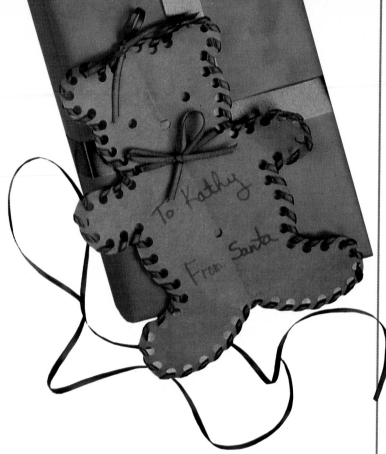

Library of Congress Catalog Card Number: 84-63033
ISBN: 0-8487-0683-8
ISSN: 0883-9085
Manufactured in the United States of America
First Printing

Executive Editor: Candace Conard Bromberg
Production Manager: Jerry Higdon
Associate Production Manager: Rick Litton
Art Director: Bob Nance

Creative Ideas for Christmas 1986

Senior Editor: Nancy Janice Fitzpatrick
Editor: Kathleen English
Assistant Editor: Alison Nichols
Foods Editor: Debby Maugans Barton
Foods Assistant: Elizabeth Jones Taliaferro
Editorial Assistant: Pamela Wheeler
Copy Chief: Mary Jean Haddin
Artists: Jane Bonds, Barbara Ball
Designer: Cindy Cooper

CONTENTS

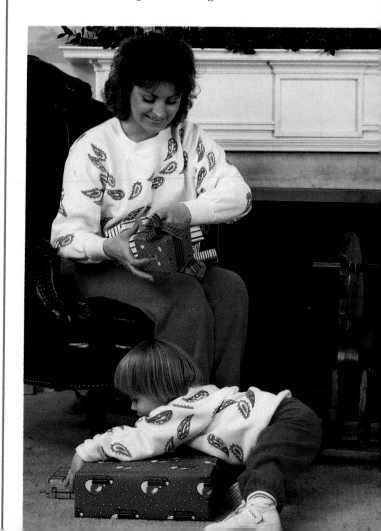

Continued

INTRODUCTION

Christmas marks the time in our lives, beating rhythm for all the turning points. A particular ornament is unpacked, and locking eyes share an insider's tale. Amassing heirlooms, great and small, begins the tale. Then add decorations that represent who you are, priceless handmade gifts, and sumptuous meals that linger long in the memory, and you have the texture of your Christmases.
Use the richness of this book to help you write 1986's chapter in your Christmas story.

HOME FOR THE HOLIDAYS

In this new chapter, three families welcome us into their festive homes, each delightfully distinguished by personal style. They have set the stage for a very special holiday by observing meaningful traditions, by finding innovative ways to decorate and entertain, and by generally adding a caring touch to all the special things they do. May their creative approach inspire the same spirit in you.

A GOOD CHRISTMAS HOUSE

Outside the window one sees mostly trees. Even during the often cold, snowy West Virginia winters, bare limbs almost obscure neighbors' homes. A narrow road winds through the valley below. Pat Bibbee points to this peaceful scene as she explains, "When my husband and I found this site, we knew that we wanted our new house to harmonize with the countryside. We didn't want to cut down a single tree unless we had to."

Opposite: Because her mother gave her the first Christmas plate when she was a senior in high school and added to them over the years, this collection is very dear to Pat. On the clock shelf is a row of birds carved by a local craftsman.

To their surprise, the Bibbees found just the right house available as a kit, a barn-like design with rustic charm. They did much of the building themselves, so that even the smallest details—an imperfect space between floorboards, or a plank with a distinctive knot—hold special meaning. In addition, Pat (an interior decorator) filled the inviting rooms with furnishings that reflect her sunny personality. With a glance around the room, Pat declares, "One of the things that I love most about this place is that it is such a good Christmas house."

Decorated for the holidays with a profusion of festive whimsy, the great room (preceding pages) proves Pat's point. Open and airy, the room admirably accepts the riotous Christmas color introduced with lots of poinsettias. A two-sided fireplace, also open to the kitchen/dining area, adds to the warmth

Above: Dressing bears for the holidays is a tradition that Pat and her daughter have shared for years. Teeny to tot-sized bears are outfitted in sweaters, scarves, and hats made of scraps.

5

and homeness of this gracious space. High raftered ceilings allow for a tall tree. And the banisters of the loft library that overlooks the great room are garlanded in pine.

Decorations, gathered over the years, fill every nook and cranny. There's a fabric tree-topper angel, a treasure found on a European vacation; a painted wooden Santa that can also double as a fireboard; a carved wooden duck; soft-sculpture characters including a Christmas bunny, a dunce-hatted gnome couple, and a rosy-cheeked Santa; and a permanent display of blue and white china plates, many with Christmas scenes. These unusual collectibles reflect Pat's fun-loving style and appreciation of crafts.

Left and below: Santa's Workshop in a wreath and the Payne Emporium, a tiny toy store, are meticulous miniature assemblages by Pat's neighbor and good friend Ann Payne. Some years ago, Ann attended a miniature workshop when she wanted to build dollhouses for her now-teenaged daughters. Her first attempt was Santa's Workshop, but she has since made many more of the diminutive and dimensional vignettes. She constructs the backdrops, does the wiring, and fashions many of the toys. She even repaints gumball machine trinkets to give them richer colors.

Above: The Bibbees make a special effort each year to photograph the family during the holidays. Since they display the photos only at Christmas, the unveiling of the festively framed images is happily anticipated each year. The children, now 12 and 15, are amused at the way they looked just a few short years ago.

Left: This handsewn gnome couple captured Pat's heart. The gnarled features of the impertinent old pair impart such impish charm, you half expect them to speak. Notice the decorative design on the shutters. Pat discovered the primitive style of a local artist and asked her to paint the shutters.

Above: Wild blueberries have yielded their moorings to the delicate crystal ornaments spangling this branch. The winding limbs were spray-painted white and then misted with artificial snow while the undercoat was still wet. Sitting atop a mirrored surface on which they shelter reindeer and other crystal figurines, the branches let fall a light dusting of their snow, further adding to the illusion of a magical winter forest.

Top right: Painted corkscrew willow radiates from a crystal vase, casting graceful heirloom ornaments high into the air in this pastel bedroom. While Christmas colors aren't called into play here, the season is beautifully evoked with snowflakes and stars, bells and balls.

BRANCH TREES BLOSSOM WITH A COLLECTION

Inside Alieze Roberts's home at Christmastime, trees of a different sort herald the season. Exquisite branch trees await discovery at almost every turn. One tree is glittering with crystal ornaments. Another holds a multitude of teddies, and yet another is softly ethereal with its lacy, elegant trimmings.

Alieze creates the trees herself, designing them as showcases for her ornaments—a collection that was born in Paris. Alieze was honeymooning in the City of Lights when a crystal ornament caught her eye. Back in the States, other ornaments took her fancy, and to exhibit her collection, she lit on the idea of displaying it on beautiful, bare limbs. Glass marbles rooted the first branch in a prized crystal vase, but eventually the collection outgrew the reach of one bough. With the passing of holidays, branch trees sprang up in room after room. Now it's a tradition.

"I want to put a tree in every main room of the house," Alieze says. "Most people just decorate the living room and dining room, but I try to carry Christmas to every room."

As she travels, Alieze gathers branches that seem well-suited to her collection. She then enlists her husband's help with painting and preparation. Friends and relatives who've seen her stunning trees make gifts of ornaments, helping her collection grow.

"Each year a great-aunt gives us a dozen snowflakes that she's crocheted," Alieze says. Those snowflakes float on the limbs of the tree in her peach and ecru bedroom. Her teddy bears liven up the den. And the first crystal ornament has been joined by many

Above: All manner of little bears cavort on winged elm limbs that reach upward from this ceramic urn. Cherubic angels, some tumbling and some holding candles, echo the ceramic of the vase and flank pictures of children in Santa's lap in this blithe tabletop scene.

others in a shimmering library display.

How does she choose her ornaments? Alieze says: "You know how you see something that you really like? I just collect them as I find them." They capture her heart, and she captures them for her collection.

9

A CUSTOM-MADE COLONIAL CHRISTMAS

Christmas is a time for sharing; not only gifts and good wishes, but also ideas and traditions. The colonial-style decorations shown on these pages—from elegant dining room arrangements featuring decorative pineapples, forced bulbs, and lots of greenery, to an inviting kitchen tree overflowing with cornhusk dolls, popcorn and cranberry garlands, gingerbread men, and beeswax candles—result from creative collaboration.

When Eve Williamson decided it was time for a new approach to Christmas decorating in her late 19th-century home, she recalled the lovely yuletide arrangements she had seen at North Carolina's Tryon Palace. She was pleasantly surprised to find that Grady Wheeler had executed the decorations. Eve had met Grady at a holiday workshop at the North Carolina Museum of History where she works as executive director. Eve sought out Grady because she knew that with their mutual appreciation and understanding of colonial and Williamsburg traditions, they could revitalize her colonial Christmas.

Eve and Grady first discussed what they felt was important to this colonial style of decorating. "I have always preferred the natural, traditional look, and I knew I wanted to display my collection of Canton china," recalls Eve. Grady suggested introducing color with baskets of amaryllis forced into bloom, and lots of greenery, taking care not to overpower the simple, colonial interior. "We knew we would use absolutely nothing artificial," explained Grady.

Right: A simple, yet dramatic, swag of boxwood and white pine frames a wreath composed of boxwood, popcorn berries, and green apples. Ginger jars on either side of the mantel overflow with decorative pineapples and poet's laurel.

Opposite: A centerpiece of palm, aucuba leaves, and decorative pineapples is a pleasant complement to this collection of Canton china. The position of the fork shows the European influence in colonial America.

He also suggested placing the Christmas tree in the kitchen, an idea Eve agreed to immediately. "Having a tree in the kitchen was such fun," Eve reminisced. "We invited so many people to our Christmas party that we served from a bedroom so the guests could mill about the kitchen and enjoy the decorations."

To keep the tree consistent with the simplicity of the colonial period, Eve and Grady used ornaments made from materials that would have been available in colonial times—mainly things associated with the preparation of food. Grady also decorated a wreath with cookies and took tradition one step further by adding lebkuchen (ginger cookies) and a molded cookie called a springerle. Both are recipes that the Pennsylvania Dutch brought from their German homeland and shared with colonial Americans.

The outcome of this team effort is a home filled to the brim with the charm and vitality of a colonial-style Christmas.

Upper left: Topping off the kitchen tree is a cranberry and popcorn starburst. Florist's wire is twisted together, spread out and threaded with popcorn and cranberries, after which the wire is knotted at the end. Later, birds will appreciate this ornament.

Left: The jaunty man in the center of the cookie wreath is a German springerle, a holiday cookie baked in a specially carved mold. Ribbon is intertwined through the grapevine wreath form. Then, lebkuchen (ginger cookies), popcorn balls, and candy canes are placed in the wreath. The cookies are decorated with cloves for extra scent.

Left: A tree and cookie wreath in the kitchen seem to say "Come on in!" With a buffet-style meal, guests enjoy the food and decorations at the same time. Graduated sizes of sugar cookies form an enticing cookie pyramid. Cookies are "glued" together with icing, and the ornamental trim is piped onto each layer, using a pastry tube or icing decorator.

Right: Wishbones, which have been cleaned and glued to florist's picks, are the surprise in this arrangement which includes cranberries threaded onto wire, and sprigs of boxwood.

WELCOME THE SEASON

Embrace all that is Christmas—candlelight and greenery, children and gifts, a general excitement that begins in November and builds with the anticipation of renewed friendships and family ties. Here, we offer a treasure trove of decorations and decorating ideas to help make this a Christmas par excellence. So, revel in the spirit, let it dazzle you, and spread the joy of celebration.

DON'T SKIMP ON THE RIBBONS

Evergreen complements any and every decor. And decorating with garlands, wreaths, and trees is one of the oldest and most appealing of all Christmas decorating customs. A trend toward embellishing traditional greenery with ribbon—lots of it, in lavish bows and rosettes and streamers of luscious moiré, taffeta, or satin—lends uncommon vivacity to these natural arrangements.

Here's the key to success with these fancy trims: don't skimp on the ribbons. Not only should you buy plenty of yardage so that your bows and streamers can be full and overlapping, but you should be sure the width of the ribbon is proportionate to these large-scale decorations. (Most of the ribbon used here is 4″ wide.) Remember, the wider the ribbon, the bigger the bow.

While red and green continue to be recognized as the traditional Christmas decorating colors, many of today's popular interior tones cannot tolerate the mix. These settings may call for a twist on tradition, and applying ribbons that match the decor to wreaths and garlands with unrestrained exuberance can provide that holiday harmony.

You may be surprised at what a profusion of streamers in exquisite turquoise, peach, fuchsia, or whatever color suits your decor, can do to transform a room into a festive, yet tasteful, celebration of the season. Moreover, the choice of ribbon can coordinate not only in color, but in style—a lively gingham says "country" loud and clear, while moiré is definitely more formal.

You can even carry your color scheme outdoors by putting ribbons on your door front or mailbox. There is a ribbon that is lined with plastic (available from most florists). It can withstand rain or snow, without

---

Preceding page: A harmonious blend of traditional greenery and a nutcracker collection dress this mantel. Massive bows frame the scene. To achieve the continuous woven-ribbon look, use several pieces of ribbon, and overlap the ends so that no breaks show.

Above: Look closely. Could that greenery really be artificial? In an arrangement which hangs over the table like this, artificial greenery is the practical choice.

Above: Douglas fir and cedar form a graceful drape for this mantel, and the warmth of the fire releases the fabulous cedar scent. To attach bows securely, fasten them with chenille stems.

drooping or losing its shape or color.

Just as your selection of ribbons can express your style, so can your choice of greenery. Use pine for an informal setting, and save the balsam, Douglas fir, or cedar to festoon your living or dining room. Keep in mind that balsam sheds less than Douglas fir, and cedar keeps its color the longest. If purchasing your greenery, check the limbs for dark green, thick needles which are certain to last the season.

Don't overlook the decorating potential of the materials found in your yard. Regional shrubs, vines, and berries add interest to arrangements, with little or no expense. Also

available is a greatly improved version of artificial greenery. Made from fabric rather than plastic, the color and shape of this greenery produce a very realistic look. Although it will always lack the intoxicating scent of real evergreen, artificial greenery is actually more practical than the real thing in certain arrangements, because it doesn't dry out or shed.

Below: Christmas needn't always be red and green or the same old mantel swag. Rather than trying to fit into that scheme, create your own tradition with immense bows, boundless streamers, even garlands hung on the diagonal.

RED AND GREEN, NATURALLY

Natural ornaments, in an abundant selection of colors, textures, and shapes, may be as close as the woods or even your own backyard. Volunteers at North Carolina's Botanical Gardens keep this in mind every January when they select a theme for their natural ornaments tree and begin looking about for materials.

This year, all ornaments were to be red and green. "Every ornament we hang is completely organic, except for the glue and the ribbon," explains the program coordinator, Dot Wilbur. The result is a Christmas tree blossoming with colorful decorations made from leaves, pods, and flowers.

Dried maple leaves dotted with tiny, red euonymus leaves are glued to a small vine wreath form. The flash of red at the bottom is dried red peppers.

Small enough to fit a wood fairy, this pair of mittens is cut from dried leaves and cuffed with rabbit tobacco flowers.

Spiky-edged strawberry leaves and dried red peppers form a lively background for clusters of rabbit tobacco flowers.

A red rose petal peeks from underneath the teardrop shapes of a sassafras leaf, and a delicate cleome blossom adds brushstrokes of white.

Colorful dogwood, sweetgum, maple, pear, and viburnum leaves form this dainty natural-leaf garland. After being dried and pressed, the leaves are glued at even intervals to a velvet ribbon.

A MERRY MITTEN QUILT

These snappy silhouettes, held high in a child's spontaneous greeting, warm the heart and wave away the cold. And since mittens are symbols of winter, conjuring images of skating on frozen ponds, throwing snowballs, and building frosty snowmen, you can display this small wall hanging all season, instead of just for the holidays.

Machine-appliquéd, a mitten at a time, and machine-quilted as well, this colorful square makes a quick impression, and a lasting one. For added interest, mittens are cut from scraps of various red and green prints.

Materials:
patterns and diagram on page 126
(*Note:* All fabrics, 100% cotton, 45" wide)
¼ yard each, white fabric, and red/green plaid fabric
⅓ yard green pin-dot and red heart print
scraps of several red prints
⅝ yard backing fabric for quilt
lightweight fusible interfacing
24" square cotton quilt batting
red, white, and green thread
transparent nylon machine-quilting thread
white typing paper
fabric glue stick

Prewash all fabrics, and be sure that they are colorfast, especially the red ones. Iron fabrics. (Pattern pieces and measurements include ¼" seam allowance.) Mitten pattern is designed for machine appliqué. To appliqué by hand, add ¼" allowance to mitten shape.

Cut pieces as follows: 8 (1½" x 45") strips green dot fabric, 4 (2½" x 45") strips red heart fabric, 24" square backing fabric, 24" square batting, 9 (4½") squares white fabric, 4 (4½") squares plaid fabric, and triangles as indicated on pattern pieces. Also cut 9 (4½") squares typing paper.

Before cutting mitten shapes from scraps of red fabric, fuse fabrics to a piece of interfacing. Transfer mitten pattern to back of interfacing, and cut out 9 mittens. Lay white fabric square on same-size paper square.

Place mitten on a white square (refer to photo), and secure in place with fabric glue stick. With a zigzag satin stitch, machine-appliqué around mitten through all layers. Tear away paper. Repeat for all 9 squares.

Follow Diagram to lay out quilt pieces. First, stitch squares together in diagonal rows. Then stitch center row to adjacent rows and press seam allowances toward darker fabric when possible. Continue, stitching outer rows to inner rows, and corner triangles to outer rows.

Right sides together, stitch green pin-dot strips to top and bottom edges of quilt. Press seams toward strips. Then, right sides facing, stitch green pin-dot strips to side edges of quilt, continuing to edge of previous strip. Trim side strips even with top and bottom strip edges, and press seams toward strips. Repeat above steps for red heart strips.

Sandwich batting between backing fabric and pieced design, wrong sides of fabric against batting. Smooth wrinkles and pin in place. (Safety pins may make basting easier.) Baste through all layers with long stitches in rows 3" apart horizontally and vertically.

With transparent nylon thread for the top thread and regular cotton sewing thread in the bobbin, machine-quilt along all assembly seams. Quilt again ¼" on either side of each seam so there are 3 parallel rows of quilting. Repeat the 3 rows of quilting from corner to corner of the plaid squares vertically and horizontally, dividing each square into fourths. Quilt around each mitten. Machine-baste ½" from outside edge of quilt, and then trim ¼" from this basting line.

To bind edges, press one long edge under ¼" on each remaining green dot strip. Right sides facing, pin unpressed edge of strips to the top and bottom edges of the quilt and stitch. Trim even with the side edges of the quilt. Fold pressed edge of strip to back of quilt, pin, and slipstitch in place. For side strips, attach as above except cover ends of binding on top and bottom. Tuck side binding ends under and slipstitch.

Note: This quilt was machine-washed and dried to give it a puffy, antique look.

THREE JOLLY SNOWMEN

This broom-waving snowman trio is made from foam-core board, a material with exciting craft potential. Rigid, yet lightweight, easy to cut, score and bend, color, and glue—it lends itself to constructions with layers and dimension. To make the happy-go-lucky threesome, cut out all three snowmen in one piece. Scoring the foam-core board between figures will allow it to bend and stand on its own. Then cut out accessories and attach them at jaunty angles.

Materials:
patterns and diagram on page 127
tracing paper (for patterns)
1 sheet (30″ x 40″) foam-core board (available at art supply stores)
craft knife (with extra blades and/or a whetstone for sharpening)
craft glue
crayons (black, red, brown)
masking tape
15 (½″) buttons

Follow Diagram to draw snowmen on tracing paper. Transfer outline to foam-core board and cut out. (*Note:* For smooth edges, use a sharp blade. Change blades often, or sharpen with a whetstone. To cut through board, make several passes rather than forcing the blade through in one motion.) As shown in Diagram, mark lines where 2 figures join, on front between first and second figures, and on back between second and third figures. Score these lines. (When scoring, cut through one layer of paper only.)

From patterns, cut out snowmen accessories and color them with a scribbling motion. Color cheeks and draw a simple red mouth as in photo. Stand snowmen, bending at scored lines. Attach small rolls of masking tape to back of cutouts and position on bodies. Lay snowmen flat and glue pieces in place—hat, boots, arms, and scarf neck first. Add scarf ends and broomsticks next, and then broom ends. Glue on buttons for buttons and eyes.

A VICTORIAN TREE: ROMANCE REMEMBERED

These decorations recall the romance of days long past when graceful swans drifted over flower-banked Victorian ponds, gentlemen went calling with bouquets in hand, and delicate ladies blushed behind elaborate fans.

On the tree skirt, seven swans swim on a blue felt field. The wreath ornament frames a swan on a mirror "pond" amid little flowers. Potpourri hearts, lacy fans, floral cornucopias, and elegant stuffed swans complete the voyage through time.

SWAN TREE SKIRT
Materials:
patterns on pages 128 and 129
2 yards (72"-wide) light blue felt
½ yard (72"-wide) white felt
½ yard (45"-wide) white lace fabric
6½ yards (2½"-wide) white gathered lace
6 yards (1"-wide) white lace
6 yards (½"-wide) white gathered lace
5 yards pink satin rattail cord
3 squares (9" x 12") green felt
7 yards (1"-wide) pink satin ribbon
1 package (100 count) 7-mm pink pom-
  poms
22" (¾"-wide) white Velcro
stuffing
craft glue

Fold blue felt in half twice to form quarters. Working from corner with no raw edges, draw a quarter-circle arc with a 36" radius. (See Diagram 1.) Pin layers together, and cut along curve with sharp scissors. For center reinforcement, draw a ring 6½" in diameter and 1" wide on blue felt (Diagram 2), and cut out. Sew this band to center of right side of skirt.

On wrong side of skirt, mark 7 points around edge, 32¼" apart. At 6 of those points, draw 13" lines toward the center of the skirt. Draw the 7th line all the way to the center. (This will be the back opening of the skirt.) Cut along this line, and cut away center fabric inside reinforcement band.

From blue felt, cut 6 pieces, 13" x 1½", and 2 pieces, 13" x ¾", for ribbon casings. On wrong side of skirt, pin the center of the 6 double casings along the 13" lines, and stitch as indicated by dotted lines in Diagram 3, leaving ends open. Stitch a single casing on each side of skirt opening at skirt edge.

Cut 3 pieces of blue felt, 22" x 1½". On wrong side of skirt, sew one of the strips to the back opening from center reinforcement to one of the single casings, stitching on both sides.

Place remaining 2 pieces together, one on top of the other, and sew seam 1/16" from edge down one long side. Place unstitched long side ½" under remaining edge of skirt opening and stitch. (See Diagram 4.) Sew Velcro on right side of these strips and wrong side of other strip to form closure.

Cut strips of the 2½" gathered lace to fit distance on edge of skirt between casings, not extending under casings, and stitch or glue to wrong side of skirt hem.

Cut 1" lace to cover stitching of casings, and stitch it to the right side of the skirt. (See Diagram 5.)

Transfer patterns for swans and wings to white felt and cut out. Pin the swans centered between casings and 11" from skirt edge, and sew to skirt.

Cut 7 (8" x 10") rectangles from lace fabric. Pin each wing face down on lace pieces. With a ⅛" seam, sew together. Trim away

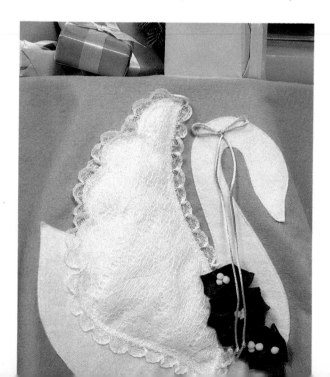

excess lace. Zigzag-stitch ½" gathered lace around edge of right side of wings. Position on swans, and sew, leaving an opening for stuffing. Stuff very lightly, and sew openings closed.

Cut the rattail cord into 7 equal pieces, make into bows, and glue to the heads of the swans where marked.

Transfer garland pattern to green felt and cut out. Gather through the center to fit area marked on pattern. Twist the garlands 1½ times, and glue to the swans' necks. Glue the 7-mm pink pompoms to each garland as shown in photo.

Cut the ribbon into 6 (32"-long) pieces and 2 (16"-long) pieces. Run the 32" pieces through the double casings. Insert the 16" pieces in the single casing, and tack at top of casing. Gather and tie ribbon into bows.

HEART POTPOURRI ORNAMENT
Materials:
pattern on page 130
5" square of blue felt
5" x 10" lace fabric
5" x 10" tulle
craft glue
½ cup potpourri
½ yard (¾"-wide) gathered nylon lace
½ yard (½"-wide) scalloped trim
½ yard (¼"-wide) braid trim for back
2½ yards (⅛"-wide) pink craft ribbon
gold thread

Transfer heart pattern to felt and cut out. Cut lace fabric and tulle into 5" squares. Glue heart to one of the pieces of lace fabric. Layer the remaining square of lace, 2 squares of tulle, and heart (lace down) as

Swan Tree Skirt

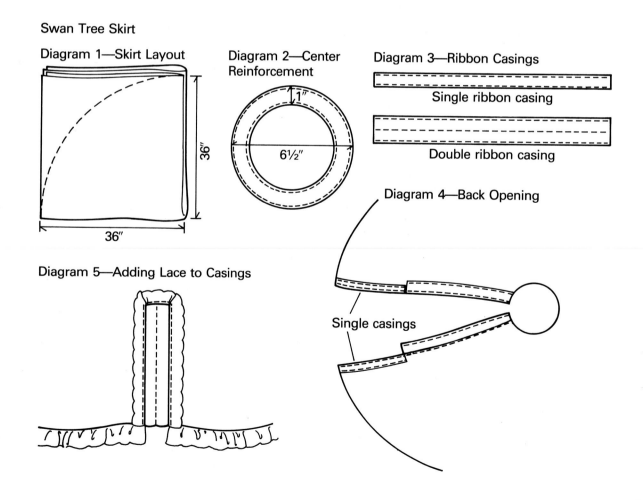

Diagram 1—Skirt Layout

Diagram 2—Center Reinforcement

Diagram 3—Ribbon Casings

Single ribbon casing

Double ribbon casing

Diagram 4—Back Opening

Single casings

Diagram 5—Adding Lace to Casings

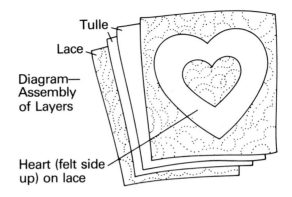

Tulle

Lace

Diagram—
Assembly
of Layers

Heart (felt side
up) on lace

shown in Diagram. Pin and zigzag-stitch around heart, leaving 3" opening. Cut away excess fabric around heart. Fill heart with potpourri between tulle layers, and stitch opening. Glue gathered lace over stitching on felt side. Glue scalloped trim over edge of lace with scallops to inside. Glue braid over stitching on back.

Make a bow as for wreath ornament, omitting hanger and adding 2 (2"-long) streamers. Glue to top front of heart. Make a hanger with a 6" loop of gold thread sewn through top center of ornament and tied.

SWAN ORNAMENT
Materials:
patterns on page 130
8" x 30" white felt
vanishing fabric marker
stuffing
6" x 10" lace fabric
1 yard (½"-wide) gathered lace
craft glue
1" x 10" green felt
6 pink 7-mm pompoms
12" pink rattail satin cord
2 pearls
gold thread

Cut an 8" x 14" piece of white felt. Fold in half (8" x 7"), and transfer swan pattern to it with vanishing marker. Sew around body line, leaving an opening in the bottom to stuff. Stuff firmly and stitch opening closed. Trim excess fabric to ⅟₁₆".

On remaining white felt, cut out 4 wings.

27

Pair pieces for 2 wings. Cut lace fabric into 2 (6" x 5") squares. Place front of each wing face down on lace square, and sew together. Trim excess lace. Sew gathered lace trim to the edge of each wing front, and pin the wing fronts and backs together, wrong sides facing. Sew together, leaving an opening for stuffing. Stuff lightly and stitch opening closed. Glue the wings to the swan as indicated on pattern.

Trim green felt with pinking shears or cut inverted scallops. Run a gathering stitch lengthwise down middle of strip, and gather to fit around neck of swan. Glue to swan, and add 3 pompoms on each side. Make a small bow with the rattail cord, and glue to front of garland. Glue pearls to swan head for eyes. Sew 6" of gold thread through top edge of swan, and tie for hanger.

WREATH ORNAMENT
Materials:
3 (13") tips of weeping birch branches
strong lightweight cord
Spanish moss
craft glue or glue gun
1¼" x 2" oval craft mirror
baby's breath, alder cones, fabric forget-me-nots, flower stamens, small ribbon roses, glazed berries
¾" plastic swan
2½ yards (⅛"-wide) blue picot ribbon
thread to match

Wrap branches into a 4" circle with tips pointing upward on the left side. Tie the bottom of wreath with cord. Glue Spanish moss to bottom, building layers, to form a nest. Glue mirror into nest, facing top of wreath. (This will be "pond" for swan.) Glue pieces of baby's breath in moss around mirror. As shown in photo, add groupings of cones, roses, flowers, stamens, and berries. Glue swan in center of mirror.

Make bow by forming several 2½" loops with blue ribbon, stitching each in center with matching thread. Make last loop 7" long for hanger. Glue bow to top of wreath, just above branch tips.

FLORAL CORNUCOPIA ORNAMENT
Materials:
pattern on page 130
6" x 8" blue felt
⅓ yard (¾"-wide) gathered lace
craft glue
⅓ yard (½"-wide) scallop trim
Spanish moss, baby's breath, 3 clusters fabric forget-me-nots
2½ yards (¼"-wide) pink craft ribbon
gold thread

Transfer pattern to felt, cut out, and stitch together. Trim seam and turn. Overlap lace on outside of cornucopia opening ¼" and glue. Glue scallop trim over the lace with scallops facing downward. Fill the felt cone with Spanish moss, and add baby's breath and forget-me-nots. Make a bow as for the wreath ornament, omitting the hanger and adding 2 (5"-long) streamers. Glue to the top front seam. Cut 6" of gold thread, stitch through the top back of the ornament, and tie for a hanger.

FAN ORNAMENT
Materials:
9½" (2½"-wide) lace
4" x 9½" blue felt
white, blue thread
9½" (1"-wide) lace
9½" (½"-wide) scalloped braid trim
craft glue
2½ yards (¼"-wide) pink craft ribbon

Pin the 2½" lace lengthwise on felt about ½" from one edge. With white thread in machine and blue thread in bobbin, sew a seam on both edges of lace. Place ¼" of the 1" lace under opposite side of felt and stitch. Glue braid over stitching flush with this edge.

When dry, press the fan in accordion pleats every ¾". Stitch through side of pleats at the end with 2½" lace to hold fan shape. Make a bow from ribbon as for the wreath ornament, omitting the hanger and adding 4 (5"-long) streamers. Glue the bow to the base of the fan.

TRIM A TABLETOP DOWEL TREE

Try this simple method to transform inexpensive wooden doweling into a Christmas tree that doesn't shed, never needs watering, and can be used year after year. The limbs of this 24" tree are made by cutting graduated lengths of doweling. After the holidays, the limbs can be removed for easy storage.

There are patterns for the apple and star tree toppers, but for a variety of additional tree toppers, use cookie cutters as your patterns. To decorate a kitchen nook, use ribbon to tie on a variety of colorful fruits. Or cut paper stars from the tree topper pattern and hang them from the limbs to make a delightful addition to a child's room.

Materials:
pattern on page 126
2' of 1¼" doweling (for center post)
drill with ⅝" and ⅜" bits
3" of ⅜" doweling
jigsaw
12½' of ⅝" doweling (for tree limbs)
2' of 1" x 12" pine shelving (this is enough for star and round base and both tree toppers)
wood glue
green, red, white, and yellow paints

Using the ⅜" bit, drill a ½" hole into the center of one end of the center post. This is the top. With the ⅝" bit, drill a 3" hole into the opposite end of center post. Cut a 3½" piece from the ⅝" doweling and glue into hole. This is the bottom.

Starting from the bottom of the center post, measure 4½" and mark. Repeat this 4 times. Drill ⅝" holes through post at each mark. Turn center post 90°. From bottom of post, measure 6¾" and mark. Mark 4½" intervals 3 more times. Drill ⅝" holes through post at these marks.

Cut the ⅝" doweling into 9 lengths: 8", 10", 12", 14", 16", 18", 20", 22", and 24". Cut a 10½" circle from the 1" pine shelving. (For optional star-shaped base, see note below.)

below.) With the ⅝" bit, drill a ½" hole in center of circular base. If desired, paint base, tree, and limbs white. Place bottom dowel of center post into circular base.

Insert dowels through the alternating holes of the center post, beginning with the 8" dowel at the top, and ending with the 24" dowel at the bottom.

Trace apple shape onto the 1" pine shelving. (For optional star top, see note below.) Cut out and paint. With the ⅜" bit, drill a ½" hole in bottom center of apple. Cut ⅜" dowel in half and glue into hole. Place apple in top hole of center post.

Note: To make optional star-shaped base, transfer star pattern to 1" pine shelving and cut out. Drill a ⅝" hole in center of star base and paint base. Insert dowel end of center post into hole of star base. To make star tree topper, trace star shape onto 1" pine shelving. Cut out and paint. Attach in same manner as apple tree topper.

HOUSE-IN-THE-SNOW STOCKING

Pieced in crisp colors of dotted swiss and polka-dot fabrics and precisely, puffily quilted, this stocking depicts a happy winter scene. A cheery house and vibrant vista sparkle on one of those brilliant days when the familiar world acquires a fresh, new look—snow-covered and sunstruck.

This stocking requires 22 patterns, but once the pieces are cut and sorted, assembly goes quickly. And if desired, you can personalize this design by substituting fabrics and trims that suggest your own abode.

Materials:
patterns on page 131
8½" x 11" (⅛" or ¼" grid) sheet graph paper (optional)
tracing paper
5" x 10½" turquoise/white dotted fabric
2½" x 13½" red check fabric
7" x 8" brown/white dotted fabric
6" x 16" red/white striped fabric (stripes parallel to 16" edge)
2½" x 4" solid red fabric
9" x 20" white dotted swiss fabric
3" x 5" solid yellow fabric
5" x 11" green/white dotted fabric
20" x 30" polyester quilt batting (traditional weight)
⅝ yard white batiste fabric (for lining)
2 yards white corded piping
zipper foot for machine
¼" diameter white shank button
2 yards white embroidery thread
4" (⅜"-wide) green grosgrain ribbon
5" (⅜"-wide) white grosgrain ribbon

Note: Finished stocking measures 13⅛" x 18½". Opening is 8½".

Although some patterns are given full-size, you will have to make some paper patterns from the following dimensions. Draw patterns (on graph paper, if available), and label with the letter and identifying tags. Cut out these pattern pieces:

A—1¼" x 8½", sky and house foundation
B—1¼" x 1¾", sky
C—1¼" x 1¼", chimney
D—1¼" x 2½", sky
E—1" x 3½", house
F—1" x 3", house
G—1" x 5", house
H—1" x 2", house and window
I—2" x 8 ½", snow
J—1½" x 3", door
K—1" x 1", window

Trace additional full-size patterns from book, and label with the letter and name of each. Paste tracing paper to medium weight paper and cut out.

To mark and cut out fabric: (*Note:* Pattern lines are stitch lines. Add ¼" seam allowance when cutting fabrics.) When transferring patterns to fabric, lay patterns face down on back of fabric, at least ½" apart so you can add ¼" seam allowance. Trace and cut out fabric pieces as follows (1 of each unless otherwise listed):

turquoise/white dotted—A, 2 B, D, L, reverse L
red check—A, 2 C
brown/white dotted—M, H, S, reverse S
red/white striped—(*Note:* horizontal means long side along stripe, vertical means short side along stripe) horizontal E, 2 vertical F, 2 horizontal G, 3 vertical H, horizontal U, horizontal reverse U, horizontal V
solid red—J
white dotted swiss—I, N, O, 2 P, Q, R, reverse R, T, reverse T
solid yellow—2 H, K
green/white dotted—3 P

To piece patches together, refer to Diagram 1 for placement and to photo for fabric colors. Starting at top of stocking and doing one row at a time, pin and stitch pieces together from left to right. Press seams open. Stitch rows together from top to bottom, and press seams open.

Lightly pencil lines for window panes.

Transfer smoke curl pattern to row above each chimney. To embroider these details, chain-stitch with 2 strands of white thread. From outline of stocking front, cut 2 same-size pieces from batting, and 3 from white batiste fabric.

Pin stocking front, right side up, to a batting piece. Baste 1/8" from edge. Trim away excess batting. Beginning at top right corner and leaving 1/2" excess, baste piping all around edge of stocking front (rolled edge of piping towards stocking and raw edges flush). Clip border just to piping to turn at top left corner. Miter at the corner formed by the toe, and at the top right corner. With zipper foot, machine-stitch.

Pin one batiste stocking shape to top edge of stocking front. Machine-stitch along previous seam for piping. Fold lining to back. Pin along edges, and then baste through layers.

To quilt stocking front, pin layers together all over the stocking. Follow Diagram 2 to hand- or machine-stitch on seam lines.

From remaining batting and batiste cut-outs, assemble stocking back same as for front, except apply piping at top edge only. Pin stocking front and back together, right sides facing. Pull any exposed piping ends toward seam allowance. Machine-stitch side and bottom edges. Trim seams, clip curves and corner at toe, and turn stocking.

Make finishing touches by hand. Tack white ribbon loop to right side of opening. Stitch on a button for a door knob. For the door wreath, sew ends of 4" green ribbon together. Gather along edge with tiny stitches. Pull thread to form wreath and tie off. Tack to door, with seam underneath.

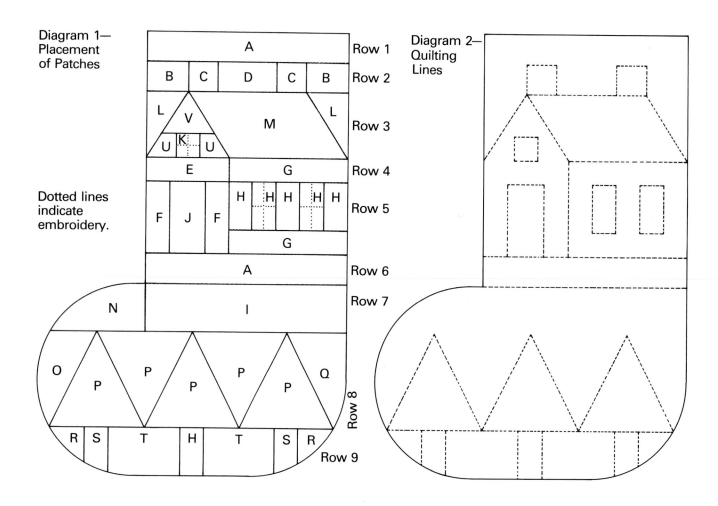

Diagram 1—Placement of Patches

Dotted lines indicate embroidery.

Diagram 2—Quilting Lines

SPRIGHTLY SANTA COUPLE

Settle Mr. and Mrs. Santa in a cheery spot, and let this sprightly couple spread smiles throughout the holidays. Mrs. Claus holds a plateful of the traditional holiday sweets, while Santa props a puppy in one hand and holds his bag of toys in the other.

These dolls are unbleached muslin, painted with acrylics, and weighted with a bag of beans for extra stability. Display them with a bit of greenery and a tiny present or two, as shown here, and they're sure to liven up your home this year.

Materials:
patterns on page 132
½ yard (45"-wide) unbleached cotton muslin
acrylic paints (red, white, yellow, green, light brown, black)
black fine-tip permanent marker
pink or light beige colored pencil
thread to match muslin
polyester stuffing
cardboard
craft glue
dried beans

For each doll, transfer pattern outline to muslin twice. Add 1" around outside of figures, and cut out. Transfer details to one pattern piece, and paint details following photo. (Tip: Test paints on muslin scrap first to check for coverage and bleeding. Then tape fabric pieces to cardboard before painting.) For Santa's gray boots and belt, use dilute black paint. When paint has dried, use black marker to outline details. Paint doll back solid red, shade face with colored pencil, and dot undiluted white paint on eyes.

With right sides facing, sew front and back of doll together, leaving bottom open. Trim seams to ¼", clip curves, and turn. Stuff firmly with polyester stuffing. Stand figure on cardboard, and trace bottom. Cut ½" inside traced line. Glue piece of muslin over one side of cardboard, overlapping ½" on the other side.

Make a small hollow in center of stuffing, and insert a bag of beans tied in a scrap of muslin. Baste along bottom edge of doll, gather stitches slightly, and tie off. Tuck ends under, and stitch muslin-covered base to doll with small overhand stitches.

For added definition, stitch through back of doll to front and then back again at points indicated on pattern, pulling stitches tight.

A HOLIDAY PARADE OF PANDAS

Choose your favorite technique from this medley of panda delights, or combine your skills to stencil, cross-stitch, and woodwork the entire set. There's not a child on anyone's gift list who wouldn't like to see his name at the top of this panda stocking. And the wooden stocking holder eliminates the need for a nail, so that the stocking may be hung from a bedroom shelf or table. Complete the panda ensemble with a fluffy yarn wreath decorated with pom-pom pandas.

WREATH
Materials:
coat hanger
3 skeins of white yarn
4" x 5" piece of stiff cardboard
sheet of black felt
12 (¾") white pom-poms
24 (1") black pom-poms
18 (⅝") black pom-poms
craft glue

Bend coat hanger into a circle, leaving top hook as hanger. Wrap 20 rounds of yarn around the 4" side of cardboard. Remove yarn bundle from cardboard. Tie a 6" length of yarn around center of gathered yarn bundle. Tie bundle to wire circle with same piece of yarn.

Using remaining yarn, repeat the gathering and tying process until wreath is full. To make pandas, cut 1½" x 2" pieces from felt and glue pom-poms to felt as shown in photograph. Let dry, trim felt backing, and glue the back of each panda to yarn wreath, at even intervals.

STOCKING
Materials:
pattern on page 134
½ yard (45"-wide) white broadcloth
permanent marker
sheet of plastic (for stencil)
craft knife
2 large stencil brushes
black, white fabric paints
8" x 5" 14-count red Aida cloth
white embroidery floss
2 yards red piping
½ yard (⅜"-wide) satin ribbon

Fold broadcloth in half, short ends together. Transfer stocking pattern to broadcloth and cut out. Transfer stencil patterns to plastic with marker and cut out. Position stencil #1 in middle of lower portion of stocking piece as shown in photo, and tape. Stencil with black paint in brushing motion and let dry. Position stencil #2 over first stenciling and using a different brush, stencil with white paint. Leave stencil #2 in place.

To create a shadowed edge around the panda body, dip the white stencil brush in a small amount of black paint and, on a piece of paper or cloth, mix the paints until a gray color develops. Using a swirling motion, paint around the #2 stencil. Remove stencil and let dry.

Cross-stitch child's name on Aida cloth (to enlarge name, cross-stitch over 2 threads rather than one). Sew piping to long sides of name section and iron seams toward back. Position name section 2¾" from top of stocking and stitch.

Stitch piping around sides and bottom of stocking front with raw edges aligned. Place stocking pieces right sides together and stitch over seam for piping. Trim seams, clip corners, and turn.

Cut a 6" length of ribbon and fold in half to form a loop. Turn top of stocking under ¼" and iron. Turn under ½" and stitch. Tack the ribbon loop on the inside right of the stocking. Tie a bow with the remaining ribbon and tack it at the bear's neck. Iron the stocking, being careful not to iron the stenciled area or name.

STOCKING HOLDER
Materials:
pattern on page 135
5½" x 9" piece of 1" pine shelving
4" x 4" piece of ⅜" wood (for arm and extended leg)
band or jigsaw
sandpaper
satin varnish
acrylic paint (red, black, and white)
paintbrushes
wood glue
wood clamps
drill with ⅜" bit
1¼" of ⅜" doweling

Transfer patterns to wood; cut out, sand, and varnish all pieces. Transfer painting details to body piece, arm, and extended leg. Paint as directed. Apply wood glue to straight edge of back support, and position on back of body piece so that bottom edges of both pieces are flush. Clamp in place for several minutes.

Drill a ¼" hole into back side of extended leg where indicated (to mark depth of hole, place a piece of tape ¼" from point of drill bit). Drip wood glue into hole and insert dowel. Apply wood glue to areas on arm and leg that will touch body piece and clamp in place for several minutes. Varnish entire piece.

SWEETNESS AND LIGHT: AN ANGEL CHOIR

Except for bits of color added with markers and candy decorations, these angel ornaments are formed entirely from white Royal Icing. The heavenly bodies are first outlined in a continuous line of icing that is allowed to dry. Then a flowing layer of the sweet stuff is used to fill in, and finally piped dots, dashes, swirls, and squiggles are added to decorate the angelic apparel.

These sugary creations are the first of several Christmas angels that you'll find on the following pages. They're made from a variety of materials—paper, wood, muslin, even baby socks—and we hope one or more will wing its way into your heart and home this holiday season.

Materials:
patterns on page 153
tracing paper
felt-tip markers (pastel colors)
white paper
parchment or waxed paper
large glass mixing bowl
electric mixer
ingredients for Royal Icing (listed below)
pastry bag with No. 2 metal tip
commercial cake-decorating candies
hot glue gun and glue sticks
ribbon or cord

Trace the outline of the angel patterns with a felt-tip marker onto tracing paper. Then transfer pattern to white paper, and tape to a smooth work surface. (Since the angels will have to dry flat for 48 hours, choose a work area that can remain undisturbed.) Place a piece of parchment or waxed paper over each pattern, and tape to secure. (You will be applying icing to this paper.)

Royal Icing:
½ teaspoon cream of tartar
3 egg whites (at room temperature)
1 (16-ounce) package powdered sugar, sifted

To prepare Royal Icing, combine cream of tartar and egg whites in a large glass mixing bowl. Beat at medium speed of electric mixer until soft peaks form. Gradually add sugar; continue beating 5 to 7 minutes or until mixture is very stiff. Royal Icing dries quickly: keep covered with damp towel.

Spoon one-third of icing into a pastry bag fitted with the No. 2 metal tip. Pipe icing in a continuous line around outline of each angel pattern. Set aside to dry.

Spoon another one-third of icing into a small mixing bowl. To make icing a good flowing consistency, add water, ½ teaspoon

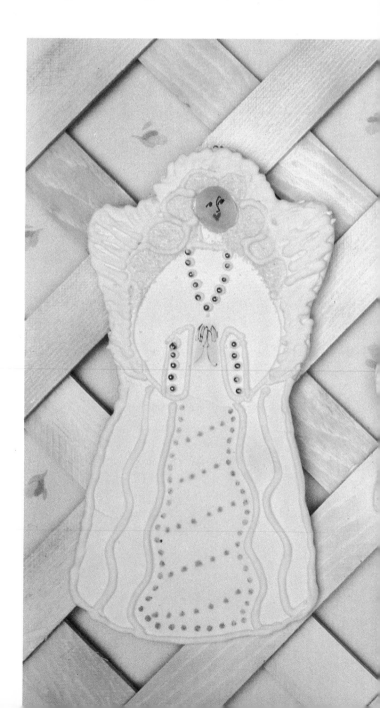

at a time. Spoon icing into a parchment cone, filling no more than half full. Snip off small tip of cone and allow icing to flow into angel outline. Spread and smooth icing with the flat part of a wooden pick. Do not use too much icing, as it will flow over edge of outline. (If icing is too watery, it will run under outline.) Repeat procedure with remaining angels and remaining diluted icing. Let angels dry at room temperature at least 24 hours or until completely dry and hard. (Cover remaining one-third of icing with a damp towel and plastic wrap; store in the refrigerator.)

Let chilled icing come to room temperature, and spoon into a pastry bag fitted with the No. 2 metal tip. Refer to photos to pipe outlines and details on each angel, placing decorator candies on angels as desired. Let angels stand at room temperature at least 24 hours or until completely dry and hard.

Carefully peel parchment paper from each angel. (Angels will be very fragile.) Using pastel-colored felt-tip markers, draw faces, hands, and other details on angel ornaments. For hangers, attach ribbon or cord to the back of each angel with a hot glue gun. Yield: 2½ dozen.

PAPER SERAPH

This fair and featherweight angel is constructed with easy techniques for cutting and shaping paper. An ethereal dress materializes as openwork stars dance around a paper cone. And wings undulate as if to fly, scored front and back for a rippling effect. Burnishing, or polishing paper to make it curve, gives arms an expressive gesture. Three dots of ink add an angelic expression.

Materials:
patterns on page 136
tracing paper
2 large sheets (one at least 20″ square) white paper (construction paper weight)
fabric tape measure
small piece (6″-square) yellow paper
craft knife
red pencil
black ink pen
craft glue
craft stick

For the angel body/dress: on white paper, draw 3 half circles from the same center point with ½″, 16½″, and 20″ diameters. Along the circumference of the 20″-diameter arc, measure 21½″. Draw a line from this point to the center. Cut along line.

At midpoint of 16½″ arc, position the star pattern touching and to the inside of this line. Transfer pattern, repeat all around line, and cut out stars. Cut out ½″ diameter arc at center. Form a cone, overlapping edges, and glue in place.

Cut out head, wings, arms, halo, and strip (¼″ x 1½″) from white paper. Cut hair from yellow paper. Ink tiny black dots for eyes and mouth, and shade cheeks with red pencil. On one side of head, glue half of hair (double lock) slightly past center, and glue single lock behind head. Repeat for other side of head, overlapping in front. (See photo.) Glue head to cone, with bottom of head ½″ below top of cone.

To attach halo: fold strip in half, and with one end at center of halo, glue half of strip to halo. With strip side facing cone, position halo to extend ½″ above top of head. Glue head to front of halo, and strip to cone.

For arms: burnish with a craft stick. (See photo.) Paper will curve toward burnished area. For hands and sleeves, burnish from back, and for back of arms burnish from the front. Wrap arms around cone beneath hair. Glue arms and hair together in back.

For wings: transfer line details (be sure they are erasable) to front and back. To shape wings, score (draw blade along surface only) on front for long lines, and on back for shorter lines. (See photo.) Bend paper away from scored lines, alternating direction for each line. Position points of wings 8″ from bottom of cone, and glue wings to seam.

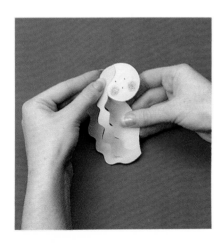

Attaching hair to head

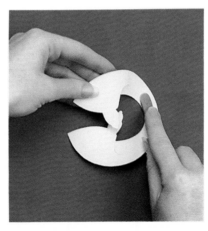

Burnishing arms

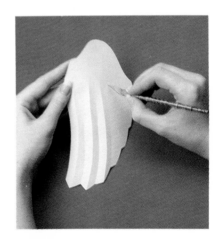

Scoring wings

A CHRISTMAS CHERUB

Floating inside a satin wreath or topping your tree, this cherubic sock angel is a treasure. Detailing on her dress echoes French hand sewing, with tiny rosebuds punctuating tucks. Swirls of ecru satin ribbon gather lace at her neck and for her halo.

She requires a sure hand, but this angel's detailing is so exquisite that she'll become a family heirloom. Even her toes are stitched and blessed with a bow. You start with a baby sock dyed with tea, and end by tying on her fluffy, scalloped wings.

Materials:

patterns on page 137
1 pair nylon baby socks (size 4-6½)
tea bag
ecru thread
polyester stuffing
dental floss or strong thin white cord
embroidery floss (lt. blue, pink, green)
red crayon
2 yards (⅛"-wide) ecru satin ribbon
¼ yard (2"-wide) gathered eyelet lace
2" x 5" piece stiff cardboard
small skein yellow angora-type yarn
wide-toothed comb
1 piece typing paper
1½ yards (¾"-wide) ecru open-weave flat
    lace
½ yard (45"-wide) ecru polyester/cotton
    fabric
6½" x 10" piece of polyester fleece
    batting
Fray Check

Dye sock light beige with tea. Rinse in cold water; lay flat to dry with heel up.

Cut all but ½" of ribbed ankle from sock. Transfer arm pattern to one side of ribbed tube; reverse; transfer to other side (see Diagram 1). Cut out; stitch hand and side seams (leaving ends open). Clip corners at thumbs, trim, and turn. Stuff arms lightly.

For legs, turn foot of sock inside out, mark a 2" line up center from toe, and stitch. Turn. Stuff legs, body, and head plumply. As

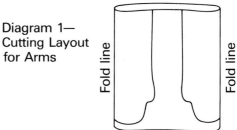

Diagram 1—
Cutting Layout
for Arms

Fold line   Fold line

you stuff, stretch sock upward to measure approximately 7". The heel of sock becomes face. Run gathering stitch along opening, and draw tightly closed, tucking sock edges to inside and securing thread.

To form neck, tightly wrap dental floss or cord ⅓ of the way from gathered top.

EYES: With light blue embroidery floss, insert needle through back of head and come out on one side of the face, as shown in photo. Make French knot, taking needle to back of head and pulling very lightly. Repeat for other eye.

MOUTH: Use pink floss, and stitch through back of head to point ½" below and centered between eyes. Make a small straight stitch to the right of center, one to the left of center, and one centered beneath the 2. Bring needle to back of head and knot. Use red crayon to rouge cheeks and brow line. Plump cheeks by inserting a needle into cheek area and pulling gently outward.

BODY DETAILS: Hand-stitch arms to body

at sides just below neck. With matching thread, come in through bottom of stitching line that divides legs, and make 4 small, puckering stitches on each foot as shown in detail photo. Add ribbon bow.

PANTIES: Cut a length of 2"-wide lace to fit around waist (bound edge of lace becomes waistband). Add ¼" seam allowance on each end of lace, and, with right sides together, stitch. Turn; slip tube over feet into position. To form crotch, hand-stitch center of front and back bottom edges together,

Diagram 2—
Making Hair

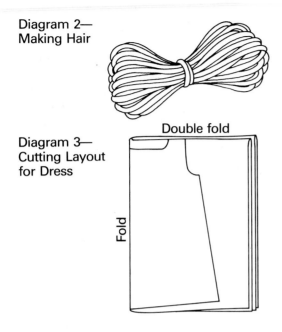

Double fold

Diagram 3—
Cutting Layout
for Dress

Fold

stitching through leg stitching. Tack waist-band to body at center back.

HAIR: Wrap yarn around length of card-board 50 times. Slip yarn from frame and tie tightly around center with doubled piece of yarn as shown in Diagram 2. Fan out evenly to make a circle, and smooth by combing with wide-toothed comb. Pin yarn circle on typing paper. Stitch ⅝" in from looped edge, tapering to ⅜" in front for bangs and widening to ⅝" again at back. Carefully tear away paper. Center wig on head so that bangs and sides frame face. With a single strand of yarn, hand-stitch hair to head along machine stitching line.

HALO: Cut a 14" length of ⅛"-wide satin ribbon, and curl with edge of scissors. Cut an 18" length of ¾"-wide flat lace. Thread ribbon through lace close to one edge. Gather lace to fit around head at stitching line. Thread one end of ribbon through a strand of yarn left of center front of hair. Tie ends of ribbon into bow; trim if needed. Distribute gathers around head.

DRESS: Cut a 13" x 18" rectangle from fabric. Fold in quarters. Transfer pattern to folded fabric as shown in Diagram 3, and cut out. Transfer marking for pin tucks on the bodice and skirt. If you have a machine

with twin needles, make pin tucks (loosen upper tension slightly and set stitch length to 1½), OR, with one needle, fold fabric on tuck lines, and sew as close to the folded edge as possible, about ¹⁄₁₆".

With 2 strands of green embroidery floss, embroider 2 small stitches for leaves at bottom of each bodice tuck. With 2 strands of pink floss, make French knots in the center of each set of leaves.

Cut a piece of lace slightly longer than neck-opening circumference. Place straight edge of lace even with cut edge of neckline, and zigzag-stitch together. Stitch lace to arm-holes the same way.

With right sides together, stitch one side seam. Stitch lace to hemline as for neckline and armholes. Press seam toward dress. Sew remaining side seam.

Cut 18" length of ribbon and curl. Starting at first bodice tuck left of center, thread ribbon through neckline lace close to seam. Put dress on angel. Draw ribbon tightly around neck, gathering lace to form neck ruffle. Tie ribbon into bow and trim if necessary.

WINGS: Cut 2 (6½" x 10") rectangles from remaining fabric and one from polyester fleece batting. Transfer wing pattern to right side of one piece of fabric. Sandwich batting between fabric, wrong sides toward batting, and pin. Starting at center bottom of wings, stitch inside pattern line, using decorative scallop stitch or machine satin stitch, around entire edge of wings. Coat stitched edge with Fray Check. Allow to dry. Trim edge close to stitching.

Cut 18" of ribbon. Stitch center of ribbon to wings where indicated on pattern, sewing through all layers. At stitching point on op-posite side, embroider 2 leaves with green floss and a French knot rosebud with pink floss. To attach wings to angel, slip ends of ribbon through armholes at back. Under front of dress, tie ribbons securely into bow on angel's tummy.

Cut 18" of ribbon for hanger. Center under wings, and bring up on either side of ribbon wing attachment (attachment will catch hanger ribbon). Tie ends into bow.

CELESTIAL CHARM CRAFTED FROM WOOD

Simple wooden cutouts and a dress of painted calico make a country angel as sweet as she is versatile. Perch her on a mantel, nestle her among greenery on a tabletop, or surround her with small candles for a centerpiece.

Materials:
patterns on page 138
2½ feet (1" x 12") pine shelving
12" x 15" (⅜"-thick) plywood
band saw or jigsaw
sandpaper
acrylic paints (red, white, black, green, yellow, blue, brown, flesh)
wood sealer
wood glue
C clamps
satin varnish

Transfer patterns for angel body and clouds to pine shelving. Transfer patterns for wreath, arms, halo, and wings to plywood. Cut out with band saw or jigsaw. Sand all edges and surfaces, and apply wood sealer. Transfer outline of face to wood and, using pattern as a guide, paint all the cut pieces. Allow to dry. Paint details on clothing and wings. Transfer facial details and hair ornament to wood, and paint. Glue pieces together as shown in photo. Clamp and let dry. Varnish entire piece.

45

ANGEL CRITTERS

Brighten your tree with a touch of angelic humor. Sparkling halos and calico dresses hemmed with lace bedeck the muslin bodies of this cat and mouse angel duo. Make both angels from one pattern, and paint their faces with permanent markers. Great to make for stocking stuffers or to give as gifts.

Materials (for each angel):
pattern on page 140
7½" x 23" piece unbleached muslin fabric
   (for body, ears, and wings)
beige thread
polyester stuffing
fine-tipped permanent marking pens
   (pink, beige, brown, black, light gray,
   and medium gray)
acrylic paint (white, brown for eyes)
paint brush (size 000)
soft red pencil
cotton fabric (for dress)
½ yard (½"-wide) ruffled lace trim
14" (¼"-wide) red ribbon
double-sided fusible web fabric
gold pipe cleaner
½ yard (1⁄16"-wide) red satin ribbon
1 black bead (for mouse nose)

To make the angel body, cut a 13½" piece from muslin. Transfer body pattern to muslin and cut out two bodies. Mark ear placement on head. Transfer ear pattern to remaining muslin and cut out 4 ears. Match ears and sew around sides, leaving bottom edge open. Trim seams, turn, and iron.

Pin ears to head on marks, with tip of ear down and raw edge of ear aligned with raw edge of head. Pin body front to back (ears will be inside) and sew edges together, leaving an opening on one side. Trim seams, clip curves and corners, turn, and iron. Stuff tightly and sew opening closed.

Note: Mouse angel is slightly different. To make mouse snout, transfer pattern to muslin and cut out two pieces. Transfer features to muslin and paint as directed. (Practice using markers on scrap muslin first, to gauge the

"bleed" of the markers.) Let dry. Sew painted sides together, trim seams, and turn. Stuff tightly. Fold raw edges under and sew to face. (See Diagram.) Sew on bead.

Transfer facial features to the doll and paint as directed. Use the beige marker to add stripes to arms and legs of cat angel. Use the light gray marker to paint the arms and legs of mouse angel, and the dark gray marker to add marks for fingers and toes. To give cheeks blush, rub lightly with the red pencil.

To make dress, fold the cotton fabric in half, short ends together, and cut on the fold. Fold each cotton piece in half, short ends together. Transfer dress pattern to one fold and cut out. Repeat on other cotton piece. Fold fabric under ¼" on the neck, sleeves, and hem of both dress pieces and iron. Pin shoulders, right sides together, and sew to neck opening. Iron seam open. Cut two 3" lengths of lace and sew to sleeves. Sew underarm and side seams using a ¼" allowance. Iron seam open. Sew remaining lace to hem. Clip dress corners and turn. Slip dress over head. Gather around the neck, and tie off in back. Tie the ¼"-wide red ribbon in a bow around the neck.

To make wings, cut two 4" x 6" pieces from muslin and fuse them together with fusible web. Transfer wing pattern to muslin and cut out. Position the center of wings on center of angel back and stitch wings to body. Fold one end of the pipe cleaner around a spool to form a halo. Cut other end of pipe cleaner to form a 4½" stem and sew to center of wings. To hang ornament, fold the 1⁄16" ribbon in half and tie ends in a knot. Sew knot to back of head.

Diagram—
Attaching
Snout to
Face

BAG A BUNCH OF BEARS

Ribbon trim and paper-punched holes will transform your ordinary, nondescript paper bags into adorable bear decorations. Three different patterns allow you to create bunches of bears—bears to hang on the tree, bear gift tags, and a continuous string of bears, joined at the paws. To make more than the four joined together in the photograph, start with a larger piece of paper and more folds. If small children are participating, an adult will need to help cut out the figures, but everyone will enjoy punching the holes and lacing the colorful ribbon. The result will be bears so charming, no one will guess their humble beginnings.

Materials (for large bear):
pattern on page 141
6" x 8" piece of brown paper bag
paper punch
2 yards (⅛"-wide) red or green satin
  ribbon
tape

Fold brown paper in half. Transfer pattern to brown paper, placing straight side on fold. Cut out. Keeping paper folded, punch holes all around edge of pattern. Punch eye hole. To punch nose and navel, position paper punch so that half is off the edge of the fold. Punch, creating a half circle.

Open bear. Cut an 11" length of ribbon and set aside. Find middle of longer ribbon length and mark lightly with a pencil. Insert ribbon into hole at bottom center of bear,

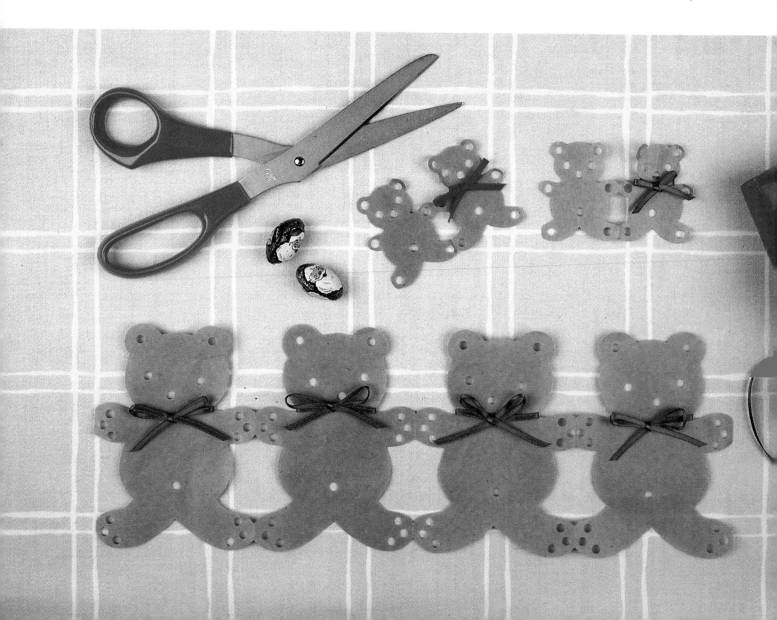

pulling it through until the center mark appears. Tape this ribbon center to back of bear at bottom hole. Begin lacing ribbon around outside of bear by coming up through a hole, over the outside and back up through the next hole, keeping ribbon smooth and untwisted as you lace. Continue to top center hole. Tape ribbon end in place at top. Remove tape from ribbon center and repeat procedure for other side. At top center of bear, untape end of ribbon and tie both ends in a bow. Tie bow around bear's neck with remaining ribbon.

Materials (for medium bears):
pattern on page 141
6″ x 15½″ plain brown bag piece
paper punch
32″ (⅛″-wide) red or green satin ribbon

Fold paper accordion-style, into equal quarters. Transfer bear pattern to folded paper, allowing paws to run off folded edges. Cut out (like paper dolls) without cutting the folds. Keeping paper folded, use paper punch to punch eyes, ears, paws, nose, and navel. Cut ribbon into four 8″ lengths. Open bears and tie ribbon around necks.

Materials (for small bears):
3″ x 4″ brown paper bag piece
paper punch
8″ (⅛″-wide) red or green satin ribbon

Fold brown paper in half. Transfer bear pattern to paper, and cut out. (Do not cut fold.) Keeping paper folded, punch holes as shown in photograph. Open bears and tie ribbon around a bear's neck.

REFLECTIONS OF THE SEASON

Light glances off the facets of these cards and decorations, making them shimmer as though made of mirrored glass. In fact, the card designs and tree with presents are made with Mirroflex, a reflective plastic that looks like glass or metal but cuts with scissors.

A mosaic effect is so easy to create with this material that children will love personalizing their cards and gift tags. You just cut out the Mirroflex, either along the lines between squares or through the squares themselves, peel off the adhesive covering on the back, and press it in place. For trickier

shapes, a little craft glue will make sure everything stays in place.

PRESENTS
Materials:
red and green Mirroflex, grid size E
gold Mirroflex, grid size M

Amount of Mirroflex needed will be determined by number and size of presents you wish to make. Cut a single piece of Mirroflex to form 4 sides of a box by bending it in 3 places as shown in Diagram 1. Remove covering and press together where 2 edges meet. Cut 2 pieces of Mirroflex to fit each end, remove covering, and press in place. Cut

length of gold Mirroflex needed to encircle box as ribbon, and attach. Form bows as for tree and attach.

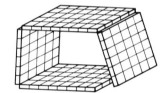

Diagram 1—
Making a Box

CARDS
Materials:
patterns on page 142
blank cards and gift tags
assorted pieces of Mirroflex (see patterns)

Enlarge or reduce patterns as needed to fit front of cards and tags. Transfer to Mirroflex, cut out, and attach to card. Follow photo for borders.

CHRISTMAS TREE
Materials:
pattern on page 142
6½" square of poster board
6" square of green Mirroflex, grid size E
craft glue
4" square of gold Mirroflex, grid size M
2" square of red Mirroflex, grid size E
2 large gold foil stars

Transfer pattern to poster board and back

of green Mirroflex and cut out. Position Mirroflex on poster board, and attach by gradually removing adhesive covering and pressing squares into place. Roll into a cone, apply craft glue to poster board tab, and glue tab edge to inside of opposite edge.

GARLAND: Spiral approximately 30" of a single row of the gold Mirroflex around tree, piecing lengths as needed. Rows should be about 1½" apart at bottom of tree and gradually decrease to about ½" at the top.

BOWS: Cut twenty-four 2½" lengths of single rows of gold Mirroflex. Remove covering and form bows as shown in Diagram 2. Attach bows to garland at approximately 1¼" intervals.

Diagram 2—
Making a Bow

ORNAMENTS: Cut out individual squares of the red Mirroflex and attach to the tree at random.

STAR: Place a large foil star on tree as shown in photo. Position remaining star on other side of tree; attach to front star at top and sides.

ORNAMENTS:
MAKE ONE, MAKE ALL

You've heard that good things come in small packages, and that is especially true of ornaments. These little decorations are versatile, serving equally well as tree trims, stocking stuffers, party favors, bazaar baubles, or package toppers. And as do-it-yourself projects, ornaments are just the right size for trying your hand at a new craft skill. Here and on the following pages is a collection in a variety of techniques.

HEART OF FELT ORNAMENT
Materials (for one ornament):
pattern on page 143
paper (for patterns)
red, green, and white felt
scissors and pinking shears
red thread
craft glue
sequins
red embroidery floss
½ yard (½"-wide) ribbon

Cut out felt shapes. Center and stack hearts on white circle. Machine-zigzag around red heart with matching thread.

Follow pattern to glue flowers, leaves, and sequins. Allow to dry. To sew white circle to red circle: Using one strand red embroidery floss and a ¼"-long running stitch, sew ⅛" inside white circle. Before finishing the circle, lightly fill ornament with stuffing. Continue stitching to close opening.

Make a hanger loop with 6" ribbon; tack to back of ornament. Tie remaining ribbon in a bow and tack in front of loop.

CHRISTMAS SEAL
Materials (for one ornament):
chart on page 143
8" square 14-count cream Aida cloth
embroidery floss (see chart, 3 yards or
   less of each color)
2 (5"-square) pieces mat board
2 (5"-square) pieces polyester fleece
calico fabric scrap (to cover back)
craft glue
½ yard red piping
½ yard (¼"-wide) white scalloped trim
½ yard (⅛"-wide) red satin ribbon

(*Note:* Use 3 strands floss for cross-stitch, and 1 strand floss for backstitch and French knots. Solid areas are cross-stitch. Lettering,

outlining, and facial features are back-stitched; eyes are cross-stitched.)

Being sure to center design on the Aida cloth, count the stitches on the chart and work the design on the cloth. Block the stitchery when complete.

Cut two 4¼" circles from mat board. Repeat for fleece. Lay stitchery face down, and center one of the mat board circles over it. Adding ½" seam allowance all around, draw around mat board on fabric and cut out. Cut calico same size as Aida cloth circle.

Place stitchery face down, lay fleece over it, and the board over the fleece. Apply glue near the edge of the board, pull cloth edges over the glue, clipping curves as necessary, and press to hold securely.

Glue piping around edge of covered circle. Glue white scalloped trim under piping. (If necessary for flexibility, clip bottom of trim.) Make a hanger loop from red satin ribbon and glue to back. For ornament back, assemble as for front, substituting calico fabric for Aida cloth. Glue front and back together. Tie a small ribbon bow with 3" streamers. Glue bow to top of ornament. Twist streamers a couple of times before gluing ends to piping.

CALICO CIRCLE BALLS

Materials (for 24 ornaments):
6 (⅛ yard each) Christmas print fabrics
craft glue
24 (3") Styrofoam balls
8 yards (¼"-wide) ribbon
pins with large colored heads

Cut 2" circles from print fabrics. For each ball, glue wrong side of fabric circles to Styrofoam ball, overlapping edges. Continue until the ball is covered. For a hanger, tie a 12" length of ribbon in a bow. Pin the bow to the ball.

PUNCHED-PAPER COVERED ORNAMENTS

Materials (for each ornament):
egg (real or plastic)
large needle
lightweight colored paper (construction paper is too heavy)
round-hole paper punch
craft glue
tweezers
cotton swabs
needle and thread
1 yard (¼"-wide) ribbon

To prepare a real egg, poke a hole in the small end with a large needle. Poke another hole in the large end and enlarge to ⅛" with the needle. Break the yolk by poking needle around inside egg. To remove contents, place mouth over small hole and blow firmly. Hold egg (large hole up) under tap and run water into egg. Blow out water. Repeat this process until water runs clear. Let egg dry overnight.

With paper punch, punch circles from colored paper. At the center of egg's small end, apply a dot of glue. (With a real egg, get as close to center as hole allows.) With tweezers, place a paper circle on glue and press to secure. (Wipe away any excess glue with a cotton swab.) Apply a thin line of glue around the first paper circle. With tweezers, place 4 or 5 circles in a row around first circle and overlapping each other like petals.

Add overlapping rows until egg is half covered. Let glue dry. Then continue rows to cover egg. Add one final circle at large end of egg.

With about 8″ of the ribbon (do not cut), make 2 loops in a figure 8 shape. Continue, adding more ribbon figure 8s, crossing at the center, and forming a bow. Stitch center to secure. Cut off excess ribbon. Glue bow center to large end of egg. For a hanger, glue a 6″ ribbon loop to bow center.

HO HO HO ORNAMENT
Materials (for one ornament):
chart on page 143
plastic canvas
red and white yarn
scraps of red and green felt
3 (⅜″) jingle bells

Follow chart to cut shape out of plastic canvas. Stitch outline of entire shape and lines between letters in white yarn. Fill in all remaining areas with red.

Cut 6 tiny holly leaves from green felt, and 6 small berries from red felt. Glue berries and leaves to Os as in photo. Tie bells at top of Os. Tie yarn hanger from back of top H and O.

LONG-STITCH CHRISTMAS TREES
Materials (for one box):
chart on page 144
6″ round wooden box
red acrylic paint
10″ square 14-count Aida cloth
embroidery floss (see chart for colors)
small gold beads
8″ square mat board
2 (8″-square) pieces batting
craft glue
20″ (¾″-wide) flat decorative ribbon
20″ red cording
10″ (¼″-wide) red picot ribbon

Paint the box and lid, and allow to dry. Center design and work long-stitch design on

Aida cloth, according to chart. Press stitchery. Sew on gold beads.

Trace lid onto mat board, batting (2 times), and stitched Aida cloth (for cloth, transfer on wrong side, and add 1" allowance). Cut out all pieces. Place stitchery face down, lay batting over it, and the mat board over the batting. Apply glue near edges of board, pull edges over glue, clipping curves as necessary, and press to secure. Glue decorative ribbon around lid rim, and glue design to top of box. Glue red cording around lid at edge. Tie a small bow from red ribbon and glue to cording at top of design.

Materials (for one ornament):
chart on page 144
8" square 14-count white Aida cloth
embroidery floss (see chart for colors)
small gold beads
2 (4"-round) pre-stick padded shapes
craft glue
8" square Christmas print fabric
18" (¼"-wide) red picot ribbon
18" red cording

Center design and work long-stitch design on Aida cloth according to chart. Press stitchery. Sew on gold beads. Trace circle form on wrong side of Aida cloth, and add 1" allowance. Cut out. Place stitchery face down and stick padded shape to it. Pull allowance to back of form, clipping curves as necessary, and glue.

For ornament back, repeat as for front, except with Christmas print material. Make a hanger loop from 7" picot ribbon. Glue to wrong side of circle, ½" from top. Glue circles together. Glue cording to outer edge of ornament. Tie a picot ribbon bow, and glue at top of ornament.

PICTURE-PERFECT PADDED FRAMES
Materials (for each ornament):
pattern on page 145
paper (for pattern)
2 (5" x 8") pieces poster board
stapler and staples
fabric scraps
felt-tip marker
quilt batting
craft glue
rickrack, buttons, ribbon, cotton ball
small photo

Transfer pattern to paper. (Do not cut out.) Lay pattern over 2 pieces of poster board and staple through layers several times inside pattern lines. Cut out on pattern outline. (Do not cut out photo opening.) Carefully remove paper pattern, leaving boards stapled together. Mark boards *front* and *back*. Remove staples. Cut photo opening from pattern, and then from poster board (front only). To make frame front, place board front right side down on wrong side of fabric. With felt-tip marker, draw outline on fabric ¾" beyond edge of board. (Do not outline photo

opening.) Cut out fabric along this line. Place poster board right side down on batting, trace exact pattern including photo opening, and cut out.

Turn batting and board front over on wrong side of fabric cutout (with batting between fabric and poster board). To secure fabric to board, pull a small section of fabric to the back and glue. Repeat on the opposite side of shape. Clipping fabric as necessary, continue attaching small sections at a time, working back and forth on opposite sides. Allow glue to dry. For photo opening, cut fabric from center to corners. Glue fabric to back of board as above.

For frame back, lay frame front on poster board back and trace photo opening. To cover this area that shows behind the photo opening, cut a piece of fabric slightly larger than the opening. Position fabric over the outline and glue in place. (If desired, frame back can be covered. Cover as for front, except omit batting and do not cut opening.) Glue on trims as desired, referring to photo for inspiration.

Lay frame front on frame back. Leaving open the area where the photograph should be inserted, glue the front to the back. For a hanger, form a loop from 6" of rickrack and glue to the top back of the frame front along the opening. Insert photograph.

CHRISTMAS COTTAGE
Materials (for each ornament)**:**
paper (for patterns)
fabric scraps
decorative trims (ribbon, lace, rickrack, beads, etc.)
fabric glue (optional)
polyester stuffing
12" (⅛"-wide) ribbon

Cut patterns from paper: a 2¾" square, a triangle 3" on all sides, and a 1¼" x 2¼" rectangle. (The patterns include a ¼" seam allowance.)

From fabric scraps, cut 7 squares (4 for walls, 1 for bottom, and 2 contrasting squares for roof). Cut 2 triangles for upper

front and back walls. Cut a rectangle for the chimney.

To make the chimney, sew short ends together, right sides facing. Turn right side out. For the roof, sew 2 squares together on one side, right sides facing, and enclosing chimney in seam (centered and raw edges flush). For front and back walls, sew triangles to squares on one side. For windows, doors, flower beds, and other decorative embellishments, glue or sew small fabric cutouts and trims to wall squares.

Sew wall squares to bottom square, right sides facing. Sew adjacent wall squares together, turning as necessary to stitch. Sew roof to front, back, and one side wall. Turn right side out through opening. Stuff cottage until firm. Hand-stitch opening closed. Stitch or glue trim around roof seams.

For a hanger, fold ribbon in half and tie a small bow near the ends. To attach the hanger, stitch through the bowknot and into the roofline of the cottage.

HANDMADE WITH LOVE

It's a thrill only a crafter knows—the look on the face of someone special who's just unwrapped a treasure wrought by loving hands, a gift that could be meant for no one else. Handmade gifts tell volumes about the care and selection that went into them, the hours spent in the making. Even little cherubs recognize the difference. Peruse the following pages—a wealth of possibilities awaits you.

A CUDDLY PILLOW OF LOVABLE LAMBS

Three fleecy sheep, on which to lay your head, will add to your comfort on those cozy winter nights spent cuddled up by the fire. This bright red, bolster-style lamb pillow is tied up with plaid ribbon and sprinkled with small gold bells.

Materials:
pattern on page 147
¼ yard unbleached muslin fabric
¼ yard fusible web fabric
1⅔ yard red fabric (36″ or 45″ width)
water-soluble fabric marker
¼ yard cream-colored fleece
cream, red thread
gray embroidery floss
3 yards (1⅜″-wide) plaid ribbon
5 (¾″) bells
3 pounds stuffing
1½ yard (¼″-wide) green grosgrain ribbon

Transfer pattern to muslin, and cut out 3 lambs. Repeat with fusible fabric. Cut a 26¾″ x 56¾″ rectangle from red fabric. Position lambs and fusible fabric on red fabric, 11″ from bottom, and 15½″ from either side. See Diagram. There should be about a 1″

space between lambs. Iron to fuse lambs to red fabric.

Using water-soluble marker, transfer face, leg, and hoof markings to each muslin lamb. Transfer body and forehead pattern to fleece and cut out 3 sets of each. Mark hind leg curve on fleece with fabric marker, and trim fleece to make a slight indentation along line, being careful not to cut through backing. Using cream-colored thread and a blind stitch, sew fleece to body and forehead of muslin sheep. Use embroidery floss to satin stitch hooves and noses. Couch muslin edges and details with embroidery floss. Right sides facing, stitch long sides of pillow. Turn.

Fold ends of red fabric under ¼″ to wrong side, and then 5¾″ to form facing for end ruffles. Iron, and stitch. See Diagram. Cut two 24″ and two 30″ lengths of plaid ribbon. Tie one 24″ length tightly around the stitching at one end. String a bell onto one end of ribbon and knot in center. Loop 30″ length of ribbon twice, and tie in the middle of the 24″ ribbon to form a bow. Stuff pillow. Repeat on other side.

Cut the green ribbon into three 18″ lengths. String a bell to the middle of the ribbon and tie a bow. Stitch bow to lamb's chin area as shown on pattern. Repeat with remaining lambs and ribbon.

Diagram—Layout for Pillow

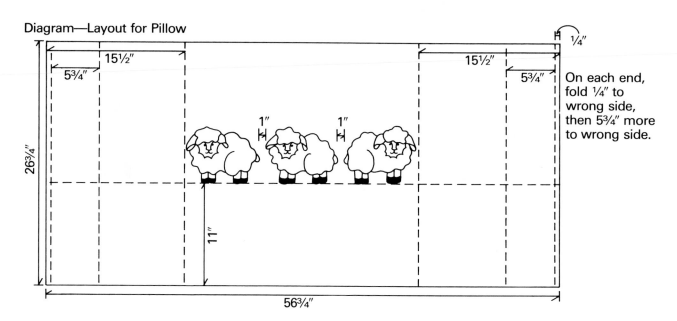

15½″   5¾″   15½″   5¾″   ¼″

1″   1″

On each end, fold ¼″ to wrong side, then 5¾″ more to wrong side.

26¾″

11″

56¾″

A STORYTELLER DOLL: THE BETTER TO CHARM WITH

Flip Red Riding Hood over, smooth back her skirt to reveal both Grandmother and the Big Bad Wolf, and see what big eyes your children have. This storyteller doll is a beautifully crafted variation on 19th-century American topsy-turvy dolls. Stitch together, in one neat package, all the story's characters, present it to a little one, and let the doll help you retell the Grimm Brothers' classic bedtime tale—the better to charm with.

Materials:

patterns on page 146
(*Note:* All fabrics, 36" wide.)
¼ yard bleached muslin
¼ yard gray muslin
black, red acrylic paint
½ yard red plaid fabric
½ yard blue calico
⅓ yard red fabric
thread to match fabrics
polyester stuffing
2 bow-shaped buttons
⅔ yard (⅛"-wide) red ribbon
brown yarn
½ yard (⅛"-wide) red and white polka-dot
  ribbon
gray yarn
1 yard (¾"-wide) nylon lace
18" (⅜"-wide) white ribbon
3 small silk flowers, small basket

Transfer patterns for arms and bodies to muslin, and cut out. Transfer and cut out Wolf's gray face and ears. With right sides facing, sew 2 halves of Wolf's face together in center front. Transfer hair placement lines and facial details to pattern pieces, and paint faces according to photos.

With right sides facing, sew side seams of ears together, turn, and press. Baste in position as shown in Diagram 1. With right sides facing, sew Wolf to piece for Red Riding Hood's back at the waist.

Sew darts on Red Riding Hood and Grandmother to shape necks. With right sides facing, sew sides of arms and hands together. Turn and stuff hands firmly, and rest of arms more loosely. Mark elbows, and sew on line, backstitching at either side. Baste in place on front of Red Riding Hood and Grandmother. Pin bodies together with right sides facing and arms and ears to inside. Grandmother and Wolf are at same end. Sew, leaving an opening for turning. Turn, stuff firmly, and blind-stitch opening closed.

DRESSES: Cut sleeves of red plaid and blue calico according to Diagram 2. Cut remaining dress pieces with the following measurements: from both red plaid and blue

calico, cut 2 sleeve cuffs 1¼" x 3½", 2 bodice pieces 2" x 7¼", 1 skirt 8" x 35", and 1 waistband 9" x 1½". From red fabric, cut a semicircle with a 12" radius. From gray fabric, cut a rectangle 6" x 18".

For each sleeve, run a gathering stitch ⅛" from edge on 10" and 5½" sides. Fold a bodice piece in matching fabric in half (to 1" x 7¼"), right side out. Gather 10" side of sleeve to 7¼", and position with bodice piece so that all raw edges are aligned. Sew together.

Fold cuff piece in half (to ⅝" x 3½"), right side out. Gather 5½" side of sleeve to 3½", and sew as for bodice piece. Turn cuff and bodice away from sleeve and press. Fold entire piece in half, right sides facing, and sew underarm seam.

Put sleeve pieces on doll, align bottom edges, and pin from bottom along front and back center edges as far toward neckline as possible. (Fabric will fold at neckline forming a shawl collar.) Blind-stitch center seams. Sew button bows on Red Riding Hood's and Grandmother's bodices as shown in photos.

With right sides facing, sew one long edge of blue and red skirt pieces together. This will be hem. Press seam open. Fold in half other direction, each skirt turned back on itself and right sides facing. Sew ends opposite fold for side seam. Refold at hem with red skirt to outside and blue skirt as lining, and press. Put red thread on sewing machine and blue in bobbin. Stitch ¼" from hem.

Working with red skirt, mark raw edge in quarters. Run a gathering stitch ⅛" from edge. Fold red waistband piece, short ends together and right sides facing, and stitch. Mark in quarters. Draw up gathered skirt to fit waistband. Pin right side of waistband to wrong side of skirt, matching quarter marks, and evenly distribute skirt gathers. Sew, bring waistband to right side of skirt, tuck remaining raw edge under ¼", and blind-stitch. Repeat for blue skirt.

Pull skirt on doll, and position each waistband as shown in photos. Tack at center front and back and on each side.

HOOD: Mark a small semicircle on hood

piece as shown in Diagram 3. Stitch a small rolled hem on curved edge of hood and a ¼" seam on straight edge. Run a gathering stitch along small semicircle, and gather to 4". Center red ribbon on right side of fabric along gathered stitching line, even gathers, and stitch.

HAIR: Draw a line down center back of

Diagram 1—Attaching Wolf's Ears

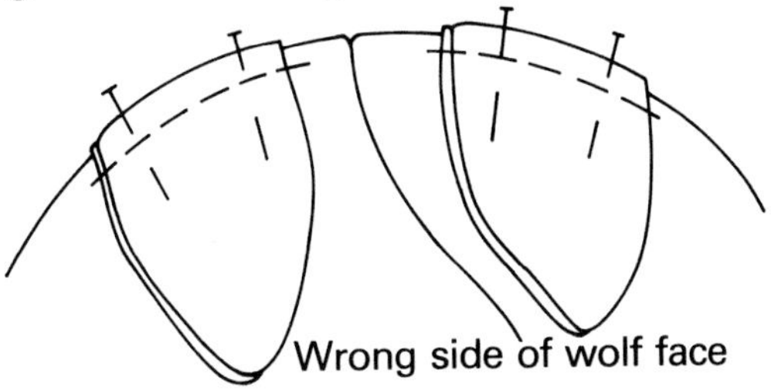

Wrong side of wolf face

Diagram 2—Pattern Dimensions for Dress Sleeve

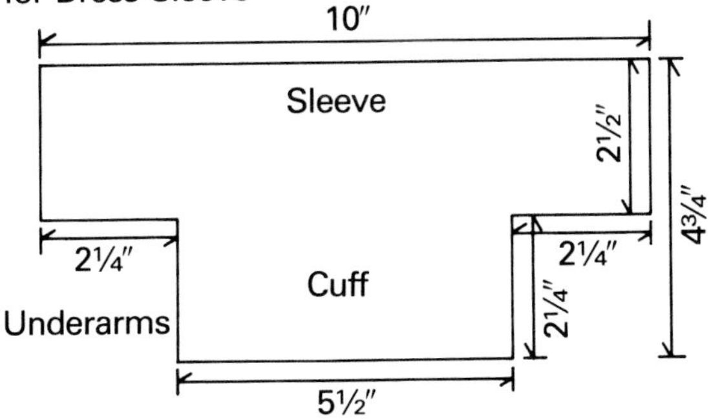

10"
Sleeve
2½"
4¾"
2¼"
2¼"
2¼"
Cuff
Underarms
5½"

Diagram 3—Hood

3½"   12"

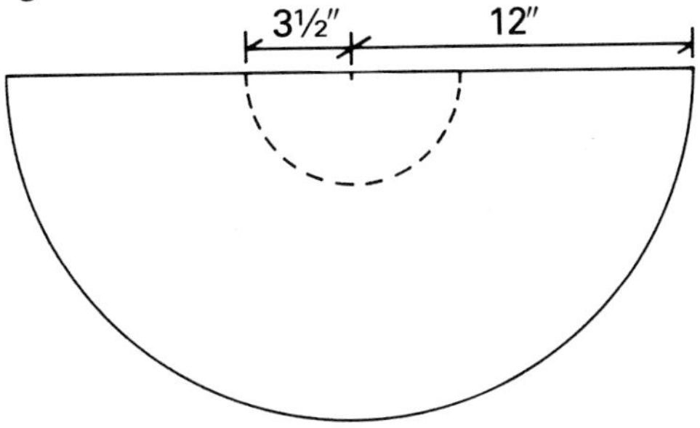

Diagram 4—Bonnet Pleats

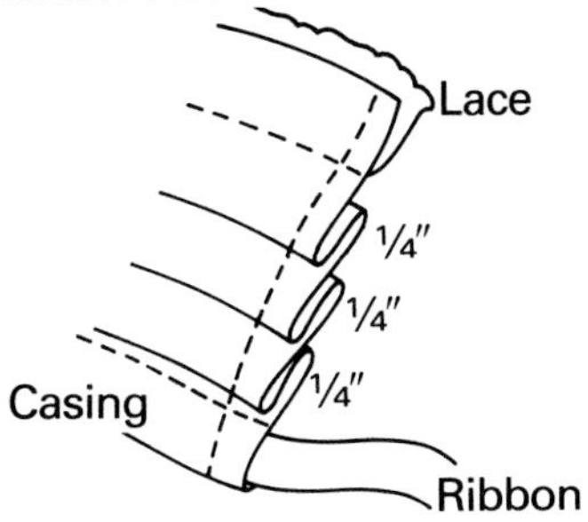

Lace
¼"
¼"
Casing   ¼"
Ribbon

Red Riding Hood's head from bang-placement line to top of center dart. For bangs, cut pieces of brown yarn 2¾ long, fold in half, and sew folded end along bang-placement line. For pigtails, cut as many 15" lengths of brown yarn as needed to cover back head along center line. Center yarn pieces on head, and stitch along center line. Gather yarn at each side of head, wrap with brown thread, and tack in place at side seam. Braid pigtails, wrap again at ends, and trim ends evenly. Tie polka-dot ribbon in bows at tied ends of each pigtail.

For Grandmother's hair, cut enough 6¼" pieces of gray yarn to fill area between seam at top of head and hair placement lines. Center pieces on head, and stitch along 2 top lines and 2 side lines. Tuck ends under, and stitch to head.

BONNET: Stitch a small rolled hem along one long side and both ends of bonnet piece. Place lace on fabric along inside of long hemmed side so that edges of fabric and lace are even. Baste together with a gathering stitch along innermost edge of lace. Lace will be next to Grandmother's face. Fold other long side of bonnet down ⅛", then fold again ½", and stitch to form casing. Thread 4½" of elastic into casing, and secure at each end, leaving casing ends open. Cut white ribbon in half, slip raw ends inside each side of casing, and stitch in place.

Make 3 pleats on ends of bonnet following Diagram 4, and stitch. Place bonnet on Grandmother's head, and gather lacy edge until bonnet fits. Using doubled thread, blind-stitch bonnet to head along seam between Grandmother's and Wolf's faces.

Gather 18" of lace to fit on bonnet at Wolf's face so that it looks like Grandmother's. Sew to Wolf between ears and bonnet. Tie ribbon in bow under Wolf's chin. Bow will stay here; Wolf changes to Grandmother by pulling elastic part of bonnet over head from one side to the other.

Finish by sewing flowers to Red Riding Hood's right hand, and, if desired, tacking basket to her other hand.

CROCHET A VEST WITH PLAYFUL CHECKS

Even if you can't be sure they wear their mittens and caps, you can help guard your children against winter chill stylishly with this bright checkerboard vest. Crocheted in sport-weight yarn, it adds that important extra layer outside and warmth inside.

The front and back panels are worked in two-color double crochet, edged with colorful single-crochet borders. Single-crochet ribbing keeps the vest snug at active waistlines, and big buttons at the shoulders slip through double-crochet stitches—there are no buttonholes to worry about. Instructions include tips on working with two colors of yarn—useful for novices and experts alike.

FINISHED SIZE: 14" x 14" without ribbing. Fits size 4-6. To enlarge, add 4 ch to beginning ch for each additional inch width needed. (Increase in multiples of 8 to keep checkered pattern symmetrical.) Work 2 rows of solid-color dc between rows 7 and 17 for each additional inch length needed.

Materials:
size F crochet hook (or size needed to obtain gauge)
1 skein each (3 oz.) sport-weight yarn in 3 colors: A (main color), B (checks), and C (accent color)
tapestry needle
4 (¾") buttons

GAUGE: 4 dc = 1", 2 rows = 1"

Note: For 2-color crochet, carry the color not in use by laying it on top of the previous row and working sts of other color over it. This way, the alternate color is always ready to pick up when needed. To change colors, begin the final dc of first color as usual; then pick up second color through the last 2 loops. Second color will show through stitches slightly: keep this in mind when choosing colors.

FRONT PANEL: *Row 1:* Using color A, ch 47, dc in 4th ch from hook, dc in each ch across (44 dc). Ch 3, turn. Attach color B. Do not break off color A. *Row 2:* Working over color B, dc in next 3 dc, (with color B, dc in next 4 dc; with color A, dc in next 4 dc) repeat pattern to end of row, ending with color A. Ch 3 using color A, turn. *Row 3:* Working over color B, dc in next 3 dc. Alternate colors A and B to repeat pattern of Row 2. Change to color B on last dc, ch 3, turn. *Row 4:* Working over color A, dc in next 3 dc, (with color A, dc in next 4 dc; with color B, dc in next 4 dc) repeat pattern to end of row, ending with color B. Ch 3 using color B, turn. *Row 5:* Working over color A, dc in next 3 dc, alternate colors B and A to repeat pattern of Row 4. Change to color A on last dc, ch 3, turn. *Row 6:* Cut off color B, leaving 2" length to be woven into work later. With color A, dc in each dc across, ch 3, turn. *Row 7– Row 17:* Repeat Row 6. *Row 18:* Repeat Row 2. *Row 19:* Repeat Row 3. *Row 20:* Repeat Row 4. *Row 21:* Repeat Row 5. *Row 22:* Repeat Row 6. Break off.

BORDER: *Row 1:* Attach color A to center dc of Row 22, ch 2, sc in next dc, sc in each dc to corner, 2 sc in corner dc, sc into each dc and each row along side, 2 sc in corner, sc in each dc to corner, 2 sc in corner sc, sc in each dc and each row along side, 2 sc in corner sc, sc in each dc across to center to join row, sl st into ch 2, break off. *Row 2:* Attach color C at a different point from last attachment. Ch 2, sc in each sc around, 2 sc in each corner, sl st to join row, break off. *Row 3:* Attach color B at a different point, repeat Row 2. *Row 4:* Attach color A at a different point, ch 3, dc in next sc, dc in each sc around square, 3 dc in each corner, sl st to join row, break off. *Row 5:* Attach color C at a different point, repeat Row 4. *Row 6:* Attach color B at a different point, repeat Row 2.

BACK PANEL: Work same as front panel.

Weave loose ends of yarn into work. Cut off excess. Block finished squares. Pin together with wrong sides facing. With color B and tapestry needle, sew squares together halfway up each side. Break off.

RIBBING: *Row 1:* Using color B, ch 10, sc in 3rd ch from hook, sc in each ch across, ch 2, turn. *Row 2:* Sc in back loop of next sc, sc in back loop of each sc across, ch 2, turn. Repeat Row 2 until ribbing measures 3" shorter than diameter of sweater. Break off.

FINISHING: Use color B yarn and tapestry needle to sew ribbing into a circle. Use contrasting thread to mark center front, back, and sides of ribbing. Mark center front and back on sweater. Match the marks on ribbing to sweater and pin to hold. Use matching thread and tapestry needle to join ribbing to sweater, easing in fullness. At each shoulder, sew a button in the corner and a button 1" from it toward neck opening. These slip between 2 dc on front panel shoulders.

Standard Crochet Abbreviations
ch - chain
dc - double crochet
sc - single crochet
sl st - slip stitch
( ) A series of steps within parentheses should be worked according to instructions that follow the parentheses.

RING AROUND THE TOYS

Use children's building blocks to create decorations for a child's room. Try the ideas shown here for a beginning, and then come up with some more of your own. And don't keep all the fun to yourself. Let your little one help make these lively constructions for his room, or to give to his friends.

To make the garland of alphabet blocks shown below, insert tiny screw eyes into opposite sides of each block; then tie on connecting ribbons. Decorate a small tree in a child's room with this colorful strand. (You can display it all year, draped from post to post at the foot of the bed, or hanging from the door knob.)

For the wreath on the opposite page, simply wrap a raffia form with ribbon, ending with a pretty bow. With a hot glue gun, attach alphabet blocks to spell out a message. Here the wreath encourages little ones to R-E-A-D. For other simple messages, try a cheery S-M-I-L-E, a welcoming H-E-L-L-O, or even a child's name, as in the ornament of stacked and hot-glued blocks on the table below.

The wreath of colorful circles, shown at left serving as a candle holder, can also hang on a wall year-round. Cut out the desired wreath shape from felt and cardboard, and glue these together for a base. Then glue brightly painted wooden construction wheels to cover the cardboard, using a hot glue gun. Stack and glue another row on top of the first layer.

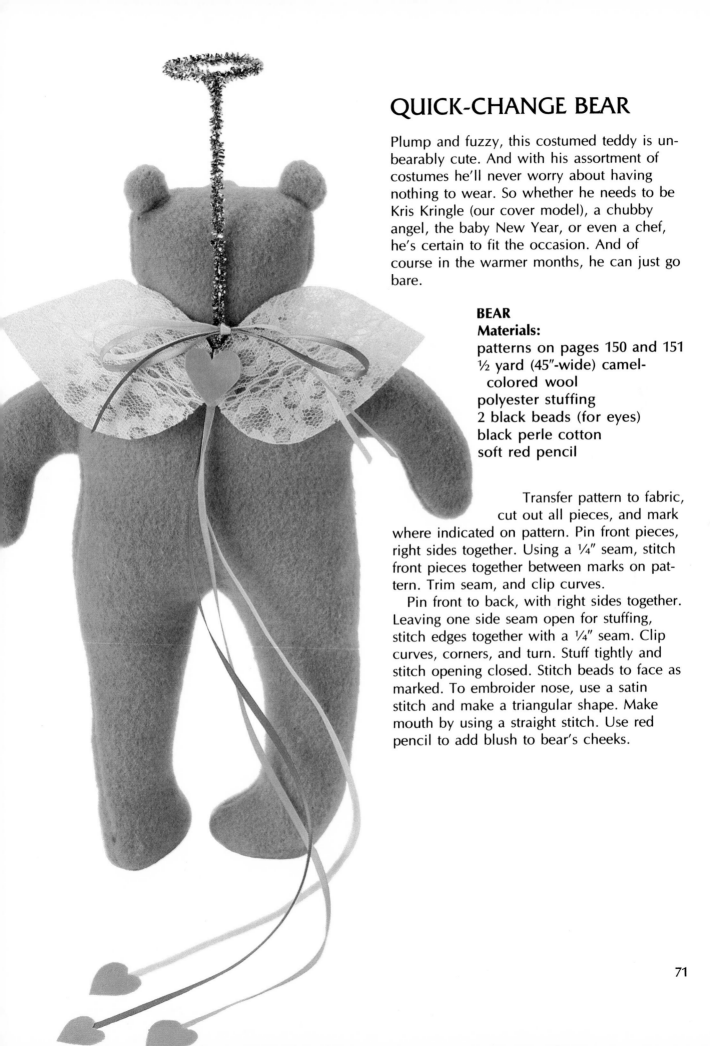

QUICK-CHANGE BEAR

Plump and fuzzy, this costumed teddy is un-bearably cute. And with his assortment of costumes he'll never worry about having nothing to wear. So whether he needs to be Kris Kringle (our cover model), a chubby angel, the baby New Year, or even a chef, he's certain to fit the occasion. And of course in the warmer months, he can just go bare.

BEAR
Materials:
patterns on pages 150 and 151
½ yard (45"-wide) camel-
  colored wool
polyester stuffing
2 black beads (for eyes)
black perle cotton
soft red pencil

Transfer pattern to fabric, cut out all pieces, and mark where indicated on pattern. Pin front pieces, right sides together. Using a ¼" seam, stitch front pieces together between marks on pattern. Trim seam, and clip curves.

Pin front to back, with right sides together. Leaving one side seam open for stuffing, stitch edges together with a ¼" seam. Clip curves, corners, and turn. Stuff tightly and stitch opening closed. Stitch beads to face as marked. To embroider nose, use a satin stitch and make a triangular shape. Make mouth by using a straight stitch. Use red pencil to add blush to bear's cheeks.

SANTA COSTUME

Materials:
⅛ yard red knit fabric
1 (1"-wide) white pom-pom
12 (½"-wide) white pom-poms
5" x 11" piece green cotton fabric
½ yard (¼"-wide) red grosgrain ribbon

To make hat, cut 2 triangles (7½" sides and a 3½" base) from knit material. With right sides facing, stitch long sides together. Fold bottom edge up ½" and stitch. Turn and stitch large pom-pom to top point. For scarf, cut a 3" x 20" length from knit material. Tack six pom-poms to each end for fringe and tie around bear's neck.

To make bag, iron short edges of green fabric under ¼" and stitch. Fold material in half, right sides and short ends together. Stitch unfinished sides and turn. Stuff with tissue or stuffing. Cut a 12" length of red ribbon and tie a bow around the top of the bag. Tack ribbon to bag at center back point. Fold remaining ribbon in half and tack ends to the back of bag for shoulder strap.

ANGEL COSTUME

Materials:
pattern on page 150
14" (4"-wide) lace ribbon
fusible web fabric
8" (1"-wide) pink satin ribbon
gold pipe cleaner
1 yard (⅛"-wide) satin ribbon in yellow, blue, and lavender
craft glue

Cut lace ribbon in half and fuse pieces together with fusible fabric. Transfer wing pattern to lace ribbon and cut out wings. Overlap center points and stitch together. Fuse 1" pink ribbon in same way as lace ribbon. Transfer heart pattern to pink ribbon and cut out 4. Glue one heart to the wing overlap.

Wrap one end of pipe cleaner around a spool to make a halo. Cut remaining stem of pipe cleaner to 5". Place pipe cleaner in center of ⅛" ribbons, wrap ribbons tightly around pipe cleaner, and stitch. Stitch wings to pipe cleaner, over ribbons. Glue remaining hearts to ribbon ends. Pin or tape wings to bear.

CHEF'S COSTUME

Materials:
¼ yard white cotton fabric
1 yard white string
red bandanna
2½" x 6" piece fusible web fabric

To make apron, cut a 5½" x 4" rectangle from the white fabric. Zigzag-stitch all edges. Turn all edges under ¼", iron, and stitch. Cut a 1¾" x 2" piece from white fabric for a pocket. Turn one edge under ¼", iron and stitch. Fold other edges under ¼" and iron. Pin pocket to right side of apron, and stitch on 3 sides close to the pocket's edges. Cut 4 pieces from string. Stitch to top and sides of apron for ties.

Cut a 2½" x 10" bias strip from the bandanna. Fold raw edges under and stitch. Tie around bear's neck.

To make chef's hat, cut a 5" x 6" length from the white fabric. Fold in half lengthwise, place fusible fabric between pieces, and fuse. Zigzag-stitch around raw edges. Fold fabric into a cylinder, overlapping edges ¼", and stitch together.

NEW YEAR'S BABY COSTUME

Materials:
15" x 7" piece white fabric
safety pin
½ yard (1½"-wide) blue satin ribbon
7 star sequins

Cut a triangle (9" sides and a 14" base) from white fabric. Fold all edges under ¼", iron, and stitch. With wrong side of diaper up, and 14" base at top, place bear on diaper. Bring side points around, center point up, and pin. Fold ribbon in half, and tack 2" from cut edges. Sew stars to ribbon.

FOLK-PAINTED HEARTS AND BEARS

Delicate flowers and hearts embellish this wooden heart-on-heart design. Bow-tied bears sit on either side of the smaller heart, reaching toward each other with outstretched paws. A light wood stain permits the natural grain of the wood to show through. And because acrylic paints dry fast, you will have this finished in no time flat.

Transfer the patterns on page 149 to a 17" piece of 1" x 12" wood, and cut out both pieces, using a band saw or jigsaw. Sand pieces, stain with a light-colored wood stain, and let dry. Using fine-tipped paintbrushes and acrylic paints, transfer painting details from pattern to wood pieces. Or, paint details freehand. When painting, use quick, simple brushstrokes to achieve the folk-art look.

After paint has dried, apply a coat of varnish and let dry. Center bears on larger heart and, using two #3 finishing nails, attach as indicated on pattern. Conceal nails with a small dab of paint, placed so that it resembles a claw. Attach a picture hanger to top back of large heart.

A WREATH FROM CURLY CEDAR SHAVINGS

This graceful, fluffy wreath is made from cedar which has been planed to form delicate, wooden curls. The spiky, dried okra pods at the center contrast with the tightly coiled cedar to make this wreath a textural and visual delight. As a bonus, cedar is a natural air freshener.

Materials:
straw wreath form
U-shaped florist's pins or hot glue gun
cedar shavings

Begin with a thin layer of cedar shavings, and attach to wreath form with pins or hot glue. Continue adding shavings until wreath is full and covered on top and sides. Add a bow or dried materials for a finishing touch.

CLEARLY CLEVER CONTAINERS

They're quick and inexpensive, and those are just two of the reasons these containers for treats are such a clever holiday idea. Versatility is another. Let this fishbowl snowman and apothecary jar candle holder add spark to a gift of goodies, shine at a church bazaar, and reflect the merriment at holiday parties.

For the snowman, choose a large goldfish bowl and a smaller one with a lip that fits snugly into the opening of the large bowl. This small bowl is the snowman's head. Follow the photograph to glue buttons and a perky straw hat on the small bowl, then fill your snowman with popcorn, white cookies, or white candies. To hold the contents neatly inside the snowman's head, cut a white cardboard circle to fit the small bowl's opening and tape it in place. Use ribbon to hide the tape, finish with a fluffy bow, and your snowman is ready for his debut.

To make the candle holder, choose an apothecary jar with a decorative, raised knob on its lid. Select a hurricane lamp chimney that fits on the lid of the jar and clears the lid's decorative knob. Use some melted wax to secure a candle to the raised knob, tie a big bow around the lamp chimney, and complete the gift with a pretty plenitude of treats or trinkets.

COOKIE CUTTERS
STAND ON THEIR OWN

Round up your Christmas cookie cutters and get ready to make much more than cookies. The familiar, festive shapes are perfect to use as ready-made patterns, and the shiny, silver metal lends a festive beginning to cookie cutter decorations. (Use care if small children are participating—the cutting edge of a cookie cutter can be sharp enough to cut a finger.)

Dress up a plain chef's apron by tracing cookie cutter shapes with permanent markers. Color some shapes solid and leave others just as outlines. Then fill in the space between the rows with free-hand zigzags or Xs. It's a colorful and charming cover for a mother's helper or an aspiring artist. (Launder anything colored with markers in a separate load for the first few washings.) Make a batch of cookies for a friend, and line the basket with a tea towel that has been decorated with corresponding cookie shapes. Cut out a cookie cutter-shaped gift tag to finish out the theme.

Cookie cutters have been filled with potpourri and are ready to be hung on the tree to sweeten the air. Choose a bright Christmas print ribbon to glue around the outside of the cookie cutters as shown in the photograph. Glue netting across one side of the cookie cutter, and cover the raw edges with silver rickrack. Then, turn the cookie cutter over, fill with potpourri, and repeat the process of attaching netting and rickrack. Make a loop hanger with leftover ribbon.

Stacked and glued and adorned with ribbon, the cookie cutters of the same shape and size become shining pyramids that stand on their own. You will need at least 10 cookie cutters with four on the base row to give the pyramid a secure foundation. Although bear and tree shapes are shown, just about any shape can be used. Before starting, try stacking the shapes, to be sure they will fit together. Glue ribbon around the outsides of the cutter shapes. Lay four cutters

down in a row on a work surface. Apply glue to two cutters at contact points, press together, and stand them upright. (This ensures that they will stand correctly.) Repeat with other two cutters and glue the two pairs together to form the bottom row. Glue second row same as first (only one less). Position on top of first row so that cutters fit in spaces between cutters of bottom row. Glue. Repeat with other rows. Place the gleaming pyramids on a kitchen countertop, mantel, or in a child's room.

Foil and basic tooling skills have transformed a pair of cookie cutters into an animated cookie cutter couple. Use an old magazine as your work surface. Cut a piece of 36-gauge foil slightly larger than the shape it is to cover. Place foil on top of the magazines and secure with tape. Press the cookie cutter down to make an outline indentation. Remove cookie cutter, and punch the foil inside this outline with a piercing tool or hammer and nail. Referring to the photo as a guide, punch decorative hearts, clothing, and faces. After punching, cut out foil around indentation and glue to cookie cutter. Cover raw edges with rickrack. Give extra personality to the couple with bright ribbon bows at their necks.

PACKAGES CAN BE PRESENTS, TOO

Amid the ripping of paper, tossing about of bows, and squeals of delight, a wrapping that is a gift in itself quietly stands out. This year, try making gift boxes to be kept.

Perhaps you know a little boy who could use a place for those extra robot parts. Maybe Grandma would love a frilly box for her growing collection of family photos. Or possibly a dear friend who loves your home-cooked goodies would also love a colorful basket. Here all the boxes sport holiday colors: personalize the shades, and you'll create a present that brings a smile of recognition even before the top is lifted.

FABRIC-COVERED BOXES
Materials:
cardboard boxes with lids
white satin fabric
various widths and colors of satin ribbon
thread to match ribbon
pearl beads
glue

For each box, measure top and sides of lid, add 1" around all sides, and cut out. Repeat for bottom. Wrap lid and bottom, separately, gluing fabric on inside of box.

For bow and pearl embellishment, fold different colors of narrow-width ribbon into several loops, tying at center. Leave long streamers. Glue bow to a corner of box, and twist streamers across as shown in photo, gluing at several points on box. Scatter pearls over knot on ribbon and along streamers, gluing in place.

For ruffles, run a gathering stitch along edge of wider width of ribbon, as close to selvage as possible. Gather to fit length of box, and secure thread. Fold ruffles loosely, tuck ends under, and stitch or glue to the box. Repeat for as many ruffles as desired.

For ribbon roses, cut 6" of wide ribbon and, following Diagram, fold ends and hand-sew a gathering stitch close to selvage. Pull

the thread and wrap the ribbon at the same time, until flower is formed. Stitch through the bottom of the flower to secure. Attach the roses where desired.

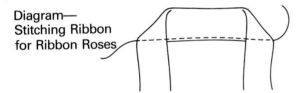

Diagram—
Stitching Ribbon
for Ribbon Roses

BOW-TOPPED BASKET
Materials:
basket with lid
white enamel spray paint
Dip 'n Drape fabric
opaque white acrylic craft paint
acrylic paints
stiff paintbrush
clear acrylic spray

Spray-paint basket white. For bow and streamers, strips of Dip 'n Drape fabric should be twice as wide as desired width and folded in half lengthwise. For bow, cut strip twice as long as desired bow size, wet double-thickness strip, fold ends to middle, and shape. Cut and wet a small piece of fabric to wrap around middle for knot, making sure it covers raw edges. Set aside.

Cut strips desired length for streamers, wet, and shape on box. Place bow on top of streamers, and allow both to dry completely.

Paint bow and streamers with 3 coats of opaque white paint, allowing paint to dry between coats. Paint desired design on bow and streamers, and paint edge of basket a coordinating color. Coat basket with clear acrylic spray.

SPONGE- AND SPATTER-PAINTED BOXES
Materials:
small wooden boxes
fine sandpaper (optional)
acrylic paints
spray enamel paints
2" square piece of household sponge

If necessary, sand boxes lightly. Paint boxes, and allow to dry thoroughly. For a varied effect in the undercoating, blend a coordinating color on parts of rims, tops, and sides.

SPONGE PAINTING: Lightly sponge acrylic paint over box, building texture gradually and evenly.

SPATTER PAINTING: Press button on spray enamel lightly to get droplets. Carefully spatter entire surface, and add colors, allowing paint to dry between coats.

PARTY EARRINGS FROM PAPER AND PAINT

You can create these attractive paper-and-paint earrings as gifts, thoughtfully reflecting the individual styles or favorite colors of the people you plan to give them to. Or treat yourself to earrings that coordinate with your holiday attire. These one-of-a-kind creations will surely garner compliments and generate conversation.

Tools needed for earring making are basic: a craft knife, scissors, artist's brushes, and a ruler. Materials include mat board or watercolor paper (the earrings' foundation), and acrylic paints. You'll also need matte or semi-gloss polymer medium (available at art supply stores) to coat all surfaces of the finished earrings to protect them from everyday exposure. Earring backs can be purchased at craft stores and affixed with epoxy glue.

Take a look at the earrings shown here for inspiration, but don't be afraid to experiment. The festive earrings pictured below are

made from mat board squares painted with white acrylic. They're embellished with serpentine (the streamers thrown at New Year's Eve celebrations), and spattered with paint. If using mat board, first cut it into the desired earring shapes—squares, rectangles, triangles, circles. Then paint all surfaces with acrylic paint. Colored or textured paper cutouts, serpentine, punched-paper circles, or other interesting materials can also be used for decoration. Experiment with the composition and attach to mat board with craft glue. If desired, accent with paint. Coat all surfaces (edges, too) of finished earrings with polymer, and attach backs with epoxy glue.

For the stylish earrings above, rectangles (2 large, 2 small) were torn from watercolor paper, dipped in water, shaped and curled with the fingers, and allowed to dry. Each piece was then painted, overpainted, and smudged and streaked with metallic acrylic paints for a marbled effect. After coating each piece with polymer, a small piece was glued on a large piece for each earring, and a back was attached with epoxy glue.

With few materials required and quick results, earring making is a perfect group project. Why not gather the ingredients and invite friends over for an earring-making party? It's bound to be a time of exciting creative exchange, and you'll all come out several pairs of earrings the richer.

PAISLEY POTATO PRINTS

Emblazen your clothing with fashionable paisley prints in bright Christmas colors, or choose your favorite color and design your own print. But don't stop with clothing. Carry the potato-print motif (page 150) to paper and create matching wrapping paper.

Be sure to put several layers of brown paper down on the work area. Then cut off one end of a potato and use a pencil to draw on it the design you want to print. Cut around the design with a knife and remove the background to make a stamp.

Mix acrylic paints with a small amount of water for a smooth consistency. Brush one paint color onto design or dip design into paint and practice stamping on newspaper. Spread the sweatshirt (or whatever you want to stamp) on a flat surface, place sheets of brown paper or cardboard between front and back of garment, and smooth out wrinkles. Print all of one color first; then wipe off potato stamp and begin with the next color. Let one side of the garment dry, turn it over, and begin again.

After the paint has thoroughly dried, place a cloth over the printed design, and iron it with a hot iron for about three minutes, to set the colors.

A FOLDER FULL OF GREETINGS

Make a friend a gift of stenciled note cards bound in a lace-trimmed folder. It's a nice way to say "Write soon!" and keeps everything needed for letter writing in one place.

Variations on the embroidered line at the bottom of the folder could include a Christmas greeting or a monogram. Slip a pen and a book of stamps inside the folder pocket for added incentive.

APPLE NOTE CARDS
Materials:
pattern on page 151
sheet of plastic (for stencils)
craft knife
blank note cards with envelopes
solid paintsticks (red, green)
¾" stencil brush
½" stencil brush

Transfer stencil patterns to plastic. Allowing 1" margin around each stencil, cut out with craft knife. Center apple stencil on note card. Using crimson paintstick, draw around outline of stencil to make a crisp edge. Apply paintstick to ¾" stencil brush and, using a circular motion, brush paint onto note card. Apply paint more heavily near edges to shade, leaving apple center lighter. Stencil leaves, using ½" stencil brush and green paintstick.

FABRIC NOTE CARD FOLDER
Materials:
pattern on page 151
¼ yard (45"-wide) muslin fabric
¼ yard (45"-wide) small print fabric
3" square of fusible web fabric
4" (¼"-wide) green ribbon
sheet of plastic (for stencil)
solid paintstick (red)
water-soluble fabric marker
7½" x 11" piece polyester batting
black embroidery floss
1⅙ yards (¾"-wide) scalloped lace
½ yard (¼"-wide) ribbon (for folder tie)

Cut one 7½" x 11" piece from muslin, and 2 pieces of the same size from print fabric for lining. Transfer apple appliqué pattern to remaining print fabric and to fusible fabric, and cut out. Pair apples and iron to fuse.

Fold muslin piece in half, short ends together, to form folder, and iron. Open folder with right side up, and pin apple appliqué to center of fabric folder, right of the fold. See Diagram. Fold green ribbon in center to form a loop leaf; then fold one end toward the center fold to form the stem. Tuck center fold and excess ribbon end under apple, as shown on Diagram and pin. Fuse the appliqué and ribbon in place by ironing.

Transfer letter *A* pattern to plastic and cut out. With paintstick, stencil *A* below appliqué and transfer phrase to fabric with water-soluble fabric marker. See Diagram.

Place folder, right side up, on batting. Align raw edges, and pin. Place a lightweight piece of paper under batting beneath apple only to stabilize stitching. Machine-appliqué apple, clip threads, and tear away paper backing. Using black floss, embroider phrase through both thicknesses. On right side of folder, align straight edge of lace with raw edge of folder (scalloped edge toward center) and baste on all sides, using a ¼" seam. Pleat the lace at the corners so that it will lie flat. Trim away excess batting.

Fold one piece of lining material in half lengthwise, wrong sides together, and iron. Align raw edges of folded piece to the long edge of the other lining piece (right side up). This becomes the pocket, and the bottom piece is the lining. Pin an end of the ribbon to each side of lining at top edge of pocket. Loop slack of ribbon in center of lining away from edges. Pin folder top to lining, right sides together, and place batting on the bottom. Stitch around edges with ¼" seam, leaving a 4½" opening for turning. Trim corners, turn, and iron. Stitch opening closed. Cut ribbon tie on angle at center. On outside of folder, topstitch ⅛" on each side of center fold. Fold at stitching and iron. Place stenciled cards in one side of pocket and envelopes in the other.

Diagram—Placement for Apple Applique and Phrase

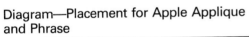
Front of folder

STENCIL, THEN QUILT, FOR PRETTY PILLOWS

These pillows delightfully illustrate what is so often typical of stenciled designs—variations on a theme. By applying four simple border patterns—varying placement and frequency, and alternating colors within a basic family—the pillows are coordinated as a set, yet each pillow is individual in design. For added textural richness, outline-quilting in matching flosses details the designs.

Materials (for one pillow):
patterns on page 148
permanent black marker
9" x 12" sheet plastic (for stencils)
craft knife
14" x 28 " piece white cotton fabric
masking tape
wax paper
5 stencil brushes (one for each color)
liquid acrylic paints (lavender, pink, yellow, light green, blue)
12" square quilt batting
embroidery floss (lavender, pink, yellow,
   light green, blue)
stuffing

To prepare stencils, trace patterns with black marker on plastic sheet, allowing 1" cutting space around each pattern. Cut along lines with knife.

Fold fabric in half. Draw a 12" square on one side of fabric. Allowing 1" extra on all sides, cut out squares. Tape one square to a flat surface, placing wax paper under the square. Find the center of the square. Follow Diagram to tape off a square.

Note: To stencil, dip the brush into the paint so that 1/4" of the bristles is covered with paint. Hold the brush vertically and tap a newspaper with an up-and-down motion (this is called stippling) until a light, even shading appears on the paper. (The brush will appear almost dry.) Use this technique to stencil each pattern.

Stencil the border between taped squares with blue. Referring to the layouts for pillows

that are shown below, draw the larger square, and tape on either side as before. Stencil with blue.

To stencil designs, work from center outward. Tape appropriate stencil in place, paint one color at a time, and allow to dry. (Refer to photo for colors.)

When pillow front is stenciled completely and dry, lay it over batting, and pin to secure. With 2 strands of matching-color floss, outline-quilt design.

Pin pillow front to back, right sides facing. With a 1" seam allowance, sew together, leaving an opening along bottom edge. Trim seam, turn, and press lightly. Stuff and sew opening closed.

Diagram 1—Taping Inner Border

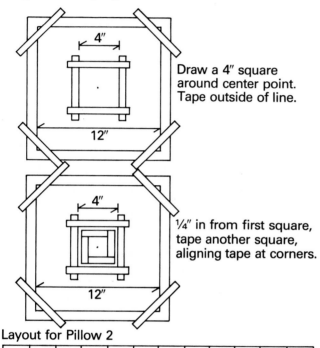

Draw a 4" square around center point. Tape outside of line.

¼" in from first square, tape another square, aligning tape at corners.

Layout for Pillow 1

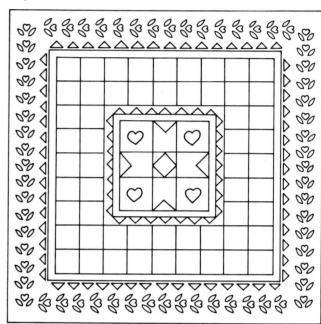

Layout for Pillow 2

Layout for Pillow 3

FROM HANDKERCHIEF TO BABY DOLL

Handkerchief baby dolls have delighted many generations of little girls. This one comes together with quick stitches and knots; then you personalize her with frilly lace and embroidered flowers.

Give her as a present, use her to top a package, or nestle her in the tree. Delicate and diaphanous, she provides a pastel counterpoint to the vivid colors of the season.

Materials:
man's white handkerchief
embroidery floss
stuffing
⅛" blue satin ribbon
¾" ecru lace

Gather center of one end of handkerchief into a ball for doll's head, and mark positions for facial features, following photo. Embroider, stuff ball, and tack to secure.

Directly under head, gather fabric into accordion folds, leaving 1½" on each side, and tack together. Tie knots in corners for hands. Tie blue ribbon in bow around neck.

Measure circumference of head, cut a piece of lace twice this long, and run a gathering stitch along one edge. Gather to fit around head as shown in photo, and blind-stitch to doll. Stitch a length of lace to opposite end of handkerchief for skirt ruffle.

Embroider a scalloped line of flowers on skirt, using lazy-daisy stitches for pink and coral petals and French knots for their blue centers. Use lazy-daisy stitches to add a cluster of blue leaves at each side.

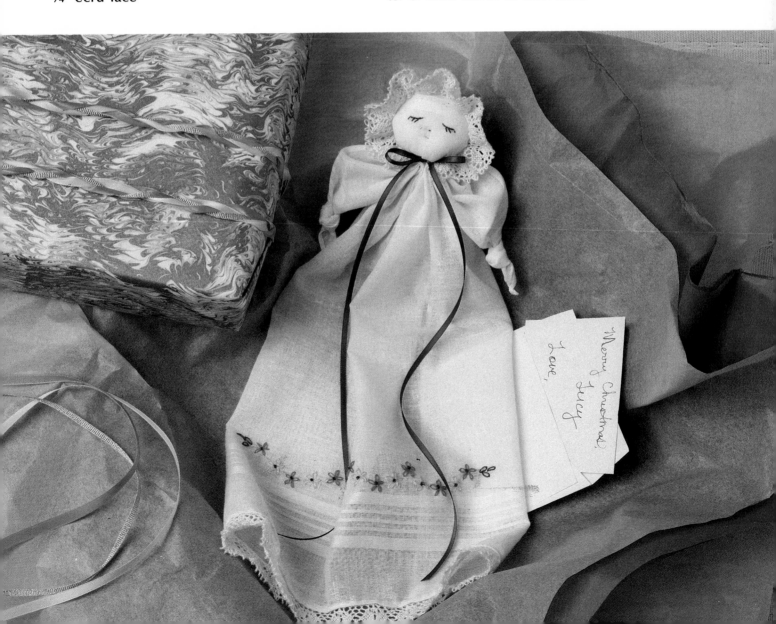

A FRAGRANT PACKAGE

Bayberry and pine, herbs and spices—Christmas, at its best, tantalizes all our senses. Stitch a muslin pillow filled with hop blossoms and soothing spices to lull the drowsy into peaceful slumber. The little pillow can be tucked between a standard pillow and its case, or shown off in a special case of its own. Package a stack of beeswax ornaments that include potpourri and drops of essential oil and imbue the air with rich and delicious fragrance.

These two wonderfully sweet-smelling presents are designed to add their voices to the symphony of the season and leave a lasting impression on fortunate recipients.

HOPS SLEEP PILLOW
Materials:
1 cup dried hop blossoms
2 teaspoons dried ground rosemary
1 teaspoon dried sweet marjoram
¼ teaspoon ground coriander
12" x 8" piece of muslin

Mix the herbs together and set them aside. (If ground rosemary and coriander are unavailable, grind whole herbs in a blender or food processor.)

Fold muslin in half (to 6" x 8"), with right sides together. Stitch with ½" seam allowance, leaving opening to turn. Turn pillow, fill with herbal mixture, and stitch closed.

Pillow may be used in pillowcase along with regular pillow or enclosed in its own small, decorative case.

BEESWAX POTPOURRI ORNAMENTS
Materials:
beeswax
potpourri
essential oil
flexible plastic candy molds

Make sure your work surface is protected from wax. Using a double boiler, or one improvised with a tin can set into an old pot, melt wax. Add 1 part potpourri to 4 parts wax, and add 4 drops of essential oil for each cup of wax. Spoon mixture into molds and refrigerate.

When cool, pop from molds. If necessary, smooth rough edges by trimming with a knife. Heat an awl, and slowly pierce holes for hangers in tops of ornaments. Add metal, cord, or ribbon hangers and bows, as desired. Be careful to store in a cool place.

PICK TULIPS
FOR THE KITCHEN

Brighten a kitchen, winter or summer, with a harvest of wooden tulip accessories. Lilting blossoms and leaves embellish this paper towel holder, napkin holder, and peg rack.

Materials:
patterns on page 152
1" x 12" pine shelving
wood doweling (various sizes)
jigsaw or band saw
drill
sandpaper
clear varnish
acrylic paints (see color key)
wood glue

Sand all wood pieces after cutting them out. After painting and assembly, finish each item with 2 coats of varnish.

PAPER TOWEL HOLDER

Transfer tulip and leaf patterns to shelving, and cut out. Cut a 7" circle from shelving. From ½" doweling, cut a piece 12½" long and one 9" long. With a ½" bit, drill ½"-deep holes in the bottoms of tulip and leaf, the center of the circle, and ½" from the edge of the circle. Paint tulip and leaf. Glue long dowel in circle's center hole. Glue one end of short dowel in leaf and other end in circle's outer hole. The tulip (placed on the long dowel) remains unglued for towel loading and removal.

NAPKIN HOLDER

Cut a 4" x 7" rectangle from shelving. Transfer tulip pattern twice to shelving, and cut out. Cut 6 pieces of ⅜" doweling 4½" long. With a ⅜" bit, drill holes ½" deep in bottom of tulip pieces where indicated on pattern. Drill corresponding holes in long sides of rectangle. Glue all pieces, as shown in photo. Seal with varnish. Transfer details to tulips and paint.

PEG RACK

Transfer pattern to shelving, and cut out. Cut 3 pieces of ¾" doweling 3½" long. With a ¾" bit, drill ½"-deep holes where indicated on pattern. Seal all pieces with varnish. Transfer details to wood and paint. Glue dowels in place.

SASHIKO STITCHING: SIMPLY BEAUTIFUL

Quilters may recognize this place mat's pattern as the Double Wedding Ring, but in Japanese Sashiko stitching, the motif is called Seven Treasures. Its geometric beauty is the product of a quick running stitch, woven along traced circles and arcs.

Materials (for 4 place mats):
diagram on page 153
⅞ yard (45"-wide) red fabric
3" square piece of cardboard
water-soluble fabric marker
white embroidery floss
red thread

Wash and iron fabric. Cut 4 pieces 14" x 20". Leave unhemmed. On cardboard, draw a circle 1¼" in diameter, and draw a cross through it, extending ½" beyond circle, to mark its quarters. To make template, cut circle out and discard. To begin the design on a mat, place the template at one corner, ½" from each edge, and trace a circle with washable marker. Draw 4 more beside it, along the long side of the rectangle. Return to edge of mat directly above this row, and draw 4 circles. Continue drawing rows, decreasing them by one circle each time, and ending with one circle on top.

Center the template on the 4 corner circles, matching the quarter-circle marks with the circles' edges. Trace an overlapping circle. Continue drawing overlapping circles along previously drawn rows. Matching quarter-circle marks along edges, make sure each circle has 4 quarter-circle arcs drawn inside of it. Add arcs as needed until corner of mat is completely filled out as shown in photo. Repeat process in opposite corner, making only 3 circles in the first row.

With white embroidery floss, sew running stitch along lines as shown in Diagram, page 153, always using enough floss to begin and end at edges of mat. Turn edges under ½" all around, covering knots in floss, and hem. Wash to remove markings.

YOUR CHRISTMAS KITCHEN

Measure, blend, and taste. Sneak a few morsels to the family pet. Pretend you don't see the surprise attack on a batch still hot from the oven. Cooking during the holidays has a reward far beyond the requirements of mere nourishment. It is a joy to be savored. Experiment with the recipes on the following pages, and once again, you'll fire the excitement unique to holiday feasting.

WRAP UP SOME HOME-COOKED GOODNESS

A dash of the cook's affection adds sweetness and spice to every gift of food. Spread holiday cheer to neighbors, teachers, friends, and associates with these dishes made in your kitchen. Tuck them in festive containers and attach a pretty bow.

CRYSTAL COOKIES
1 (8-ounce package) sourball candies
½ cup butter or margarine, softened
1 cup sugar
1 egg, lightly beaten
1 tablespoon milk
1 teaspoon vanilla extract
2¼ cups all-purpose flour
1 teaspoon baking powder
½ teaspoon salt

Sort candies according to color; crush each color separately, and set aside.

Cream butter; gradually add sugar, beating well. Add next 3 ingredients; mix well.

Combine the dry ingredients; gradually add to the creamed mixture, mixing well after each addition.

Roll dough to ¼-inch thickness on a lightly floured surface. Cut dough with 3-inch round cookie cutter. Place on lightly greased cookie sheets. Spoon 1 tablespoon crushed candy on each cookie. Bake at 350° for 10 minutes or until edges are lightly browned. Cool completely on a wire rack. Store cookies in an airtight container. Yield: about 2½ dozen.

Preceding pages: Sweet Brioche, a rich buttery bread, is glazed with jam and dusted with sugar.

Opposite: Decorative toppings and delicious ingredients make these cookies and candies perfect gifts. Clockwise from right: Lemon Hazelnut Tea Cookies, Crystal Cookies, and Orange-Date Candies (some drizzled with chocolate).

BLUEBERRY SPICE SYRUP
4 cups fresh or frozen blueberries
3 cups water, divided
Grated rind of 1 lemon
2 (3-inch) cinnamon sticks, broken in half
1 teaspoon whole cloves
3 cups sugar
1 tablespoon lemon juice

Combine blueberries, 2 cups water, lemon rind, cinnamon, and cloves in a large saucepan. Cover and bring to a boil. Reduce heat, and simmer 5 minutes. Strain mixture through a sieve, discarding blueberry pulp and whole spices. Set blueberry liquid aside.

Combine remaining 1 cup water and sugar in a clean saucepan; cook over medium heat, stirring frequently, until sugar dissolves. Cover and bring to a boil; uncover and stir in reserved blueberry liquid. Boil, stirring frequently, 20 minutes or until thickened. Remove from heat, and cool completely. Stir in lemon juice. Serve over pancakes or waffles. Yield: about 3 cups.

ORANGE-DATE CANDIES
Grated rind of 1 large orange
2 teaspoons Grand Marnier or other orange-flavored liqueur
2 tablespoons butter or margarine, softened
1 egg yolk
2 tablespoons slivered almonds, toasted
3 (1-ounce) squares semisweet chocolate, melted and cooled
2 (8-ounce) packages pitted whole dates
1 pound commercial dipping white chocolate
Additional semisweet chocolate, melted (optional)

Combine orange rind and liqueur in a small bowl; cover and let stand 30 minutes.

Combine butter, egg yolk, almonds, and orange rind mixture in an electric blender container; process until well blended. With blender running, add 3 ounces melted chocolate, 1 tablespoon at a time, processing

until mixture is smooth. Spoon chocolate mixture into a small bowl; cover and refrigerate until firm (about 1 hour).

Using a small sharp knife, make a slit lengthwise down side of each date. Remove chocolate mixture from refrigerator and beat with electric mixer until smooth, if necessary. Spoon into a pastry bag. Pipe filling down center of each date. Press date closed, wiping any excess filling from surface of date. Repeat procedure using remaining dates and filling. Refrigerate 30 minutes.

Place dipping white chocolate in a glass or stoneware bowl that has been placed over hot water. Stir until chocolate melts. Using 2 forks, quickly dip dates, one at a time, into melted chocolate. Place on waxed paper; cool until firm. Drizzle candy with additional melted semisweet chocolate, if desired. Refrigerate in airtight containers. Yield: 5½ dozen.

PROCESSOR SWEET BRIOCHE
1 package dry yeast
⅓ cup sugar, divided
⅓ cup warm water (105° to 115°)
3 cups unbleached flour
1 teaspoon salt
3 eggs
¾ cup butter, softened
Orange marmalade or apricot jam, melted
  (optional)
Sifted powdered sugar (optional)

Dissolve yeast and 1 teaspoon sugar in warm water in a 2-cup liquid measure; let stand 5 minutes or until bubbly.

Combine flour, salt, and remaining sugar in a food processor bowl fitted with steel chopping blade; process until combined. Add dissolved yeast and eggs; process 15 seconds (dough will be soft and sticky).

Transfer dough to a large bowl. Work softened butter into dough with the back of a wooden spoon. Cover dough with a damp cloth, and let rise in a warm place (85°), free from drafts, 1 hour or until it has doubled in bulk. Stir the dough down; cover it with

plastic wrap, and refrigerate overnight.

Punch dough down, and turn out onto a lightly floured surface; knead 4 to 5 times. Set one-fourth of dough aside. Shape remaining dough into a ball, and place in a well-greased 5-cup brioche mold.

Shape reserved portion of dough into a ball, and shape edge to form a tapered, teardrop shape. Set aside.

Using three floured fingers, press down into center of dough in brioche mold, touching bottom of mold. Enlarge this cavity to shape of tapered end of reserved dough ball. Place tapered end in cavity, rounding upper portion of teardrop to form a smooth ball. Cover and let rise in a warm place (85°), free from drafts, 1 hour or until doubled in bulk.

Bake at 350° for 55 minutes or until golden brown. Remove bread from mold immediately, and cool on a wire rack.

Brush surface of brioche with jam, and sprinkle generously with powdered sugar, if desired. Yield: 1 loaf.

HOLIDAY TEA
8 ounces orange-pekoe tea leaves
¼ cup finely diced orange rind
2 tablespoons dried mint leaves
1 tablespoon grated lemon rind
3 (3-inch) cinnamon sticks, finely crushed

Combine all ingredients, stirring until well blended. Refrigerate tea in an airtight container up to one month. Use 1 teaspoon tea per 1 cup boiling water. Cover and steep 4 to 5 minutes. Yield: about 3½ cups.

PEPPERMINT POUND CAKE
¼ cup butter or margarine
2 eggs, beaten
½ cup water
½ to ¾ teaspoon peppermint extract
1 (16-ounce) package pound cake mix
12 drops red food coloring
Best-Ever Fudge Sauce (recipe follows)

Cream butter in a large mixing bowl; add

Above: Mint and chocolate are a winning combination in Peppermint Pound Cake with Best-Ever Fudge Sauce.

eggs, one at a time, beating well after each addition. Add water and peppermint extract, beating well. Add pound cake mix, and beat at medium speed of an electric mixer 3 minutes, scraping bowl often.

Spoon batter into a well-greased and floured 5-cup Bundt pan. Drop red food coloring over surface of batter; stir gently, using a spatula just to swirl color. Bake at 350° for 35 minutes or until a wooden pick inserted in center comes out clean. Cool cake in pan 10 minutes; remove from pan, and allow to cool completely on wire rack. Serve slices with Best-Ever Fudge Sauce. Yield: one 8-inch cake.

Best-Ever Fudge Sauce:
4 (1-ounce) squares unsweetened chocolate
¾ cup milk or half-and-half
1 cup sugar
Dash of salt
¼ cup plus 2 tablespoons butter or margarine, cut into pieces

Combine chocolate and milk in top of a double boiler. Place over simmering water, and stir frequently until mixture is smooth. Stir in sugar and salt; cook, stirring constantly, about 5 minutes or until sugar has dissolved and mixture is slightly thickened. Remove top of double boiler, and add butter; stir gently until butter melts. Serve warm; or cool completely, and spoon into decorative jars. Cover tightly, and refrigerate up to 3 weeks. Yield: 2½ cups.

CAJUN COMBO

2 tablespoons butter or margarine, melted
1 teaspoon hot sauce
1 cup roasted cashews
1 cup walnut or pecan halves
1 cup small oyster crackers
2 teaspoons chili powder
½ teaspoon garlic powder
½ teaspoon red pepper
¼ teaspoon salt

Combine butter and hot sauce in a 13- x 9- x 2-inch baking pan; add next 3 ingredients, stirring until well coated. Combine remaining ingredients, and sprinkle over nut mixture, tossing gently until well combined.

Bake at 325° for 10 minutes. Stir well, and bake 10 additional minutes. Cool completely, and store in an airtight container. Yield: 3 cups.

Microwave Conversion:

Assemble nut mixture as directed above, in a 12- x 8- x 2-inch glass baking dish.

Microwave at HIGH 6 to 8 minutes, stirring every 2 minutes. Cool completely, and store in an airtight container.

LEMON HAZELNUT TEA COOKIES

1¼ cups all-purpose flour
¾ cup plus 3 tablespoons sugar, divided
4 ounces shelled hazelnuts, ground
⅔ cup butter or margarine, divided and
   softened
1 egg yolk
2 tablespoons water
1 teaspoon grated lemon rind
¼ cup plus 2 tablespoons freshly
   squeezed lemon juice
3 eggs

Combine flour, 3 tablespoons sugar, and hazelnuts in a medium mixing bowl. Cut 6 tablespoons butter into flour mixture with a pastry blender until mixture resembles coarse meal. Combine egg yolk and water, stirring with a fork until blended. Add yolk mixture to dry ingredients, stirring with a fork just

until dry ingredients are moistened.

Turn dough out onto a floured surface; knead until smooth (about 1 minute). Divide dough in half. Press half of dough evenly into bottom of a greased 13- x 9- x 2-inch baking pan; set aside. Wrap remaining dough in plastic wrap, and refrigerate.

Cream remaining 4⅔ tablespoons butter in a small mixing bowl; gradually add remaining ¾ cup sugar, beating until light and fluffy. Add lemon rind, lemon juice, and eggs, beating well (mixture will appear curdled). Spread lemon mixture evenly over dough. Crumble remaining chilled dough over lemon filling.

Bake at 375° for 35 minutes or until lightly browned. Cool completely in pan on a wire rack. Cut into 2-inch squares, and cut each square in half to form triangles. Yield: 4 dozen triangles.

LEMON-BASIL VINAIGRETTE

1 tablespoon coarse ground mustard
2 cloves garlic
1 teaspoon freshly ground pepper
¾ teaspoon dried basil leaves
½ teaspoon salt
¼ cup fresh lemon juice
1¼ cups olive oil
2 tablespoons white wine vinegar

Combine first 6 ingredients, stirring until well blended. Gradually add olive oil and vinegar, whisking constantly.

Pour vinaigrette in a decorative glass jar; cover tightly, and refrigerate up to 1 month. Shake before serving. Yield: 1⅔ cups.

POTTED CURRY SPREAD

½ cup butter or margarine
4 cups (1 pound) finely shredded sharp
   Cheddar, Gouda, or Monterey Jack
   cheese
¼ cup brandy
1 teaspoon curry powder
¼ teaspoon red pepper
½ cup finely minced pepperoni or ham

Cream butter in a large mixing bowl; add cheese, and beat until well blended. Add remaining ingredients, beating well. Spoon cheese mixture into individual custard cups, ramekins, or small clay pots. Cover with plastic wrap, and refrigerate overnight.

Serve at room temperature with crackers or breadsticks. Yield: 2½ cups.

BRICKLE
CAKE SQUARES
1 cup butter or margarine, divided and
    softened
¾ cup sugar
4 eggs
2 teaspoons vanilla extract, divided
2 cups all-purpose flour, divided
⅓ cup cocoa
½ teaspoon soda, divided
½ teaspoon salt, divided
1 (6-ounce) package almond brickle chips,
    divided
¾ cup firmly packed brown sugar

Cream ½ cup butter in a medium mixing bowl; gradually add sugar, beating until light and fluffy. Add 2 eggs, one at a time, beating well after each addition. Stir in 1 teaspoon vanilla. Combine 1 cup flour, cocoa, ¼ teaspoon soda, ¼ teaspoon salt, and ½ cup plus 2 tablespoons almond brickle chips in a small mixing bowl; add to creamed mixture, stirring well.

Spread mixture evenly in a well-greased 9-inch square baking pan. Bake at 350° for 20 to 22 minutes. Cool completely, and cut into 2¼-inch squares. Set aside.

Cream remaining butter in a medium mixing bowl; gradually add brown sugar, beating until light and fluffy. Add remaining 2 eggs, one at a time, beating well after each addition. Stir in remaining vanilla. Combine remaining 1 cup flour, ¼ teaspoon soda, ¼ teaspoon salt, and 5 tablespoons almond brickle chips in a small mixing bowl; add to creamed mixture, stirring well.

Spread the mixture evenly in a well-greased 9-inch square baking pan. Sprinkle the remaining brickle chips evenly over the mixture. Bake at 350° for 20 to 22 minutes. Cool completely, and cut into 2¼-inch squares. Arrange the brownies in a checkerboard design on a serving platter or in a gift box, and wrap them securely in plastic wrap. Yield: 2½ dozen.

ORANGE-ZUCCHINI BREAD
4 eggs
2 cups sugar
1⅓ cups vegetable oil
2 tablespoons grated orange rind
1 tablespoon plus 1 teaspoon vanilla
    extract
3 cups shredded zucchini
1⅓ cups chopped walnuts or pecans
4 cups all-purpose flour
1 tablespoon ground cinnamon
1 teaspoon baking powder
1 teaspoon soda
1 teaspoon salt
Orange Glaze (recipe follows)

Combine first 5 ingredients in a large mixing bowl; beat at medium speed of an electric mixer until well blended. Stir in zucchini and walnuts. Combine flour, cinnamon, baking powder, soda, and salt in a small bowl; stir well. Add dry ingredients to zucchini mixture, stirring just until moistened.

Spoon batter into 2 greased and floured 9- x 5- x 3-inch loafpans. Bake at 350° for 1 hour or until wooden pick inserted in center comes out clean. Cool in pans 10 minutes; remove from pans, and cool completely on wire racks. Drizzle with Orange Glaze, if desired. Yield: 2 loaves.

Orange Glaze:
1 cup sifted powdered sugar
1 tablespoon orange juice
2 tablespoons Triple Sec or other
    orange-flavored liqueur

Combine all ingredients in a small mixing bowl, stirring until smooth. Drizzle glaze over bread loaves. Yield: about ⅓ cup.

ENTERTAINING DESSERTS

WHITE FUDGE TERRINE
MERINGUE STICKS
GINGERED CHOCOLATE CREAM
PRALINE LAYER CAKE
OLD-FASHIONED FRUIT TORTE
SPECIAL PINEAPPLE CHEESECAKE
CHERRY FRUITCAKES
BLUE CHEESE SPREAD
WITH ALMOND RUSKS AND APPLE WEDGES
SPARKLING PUNCH
COFFEE BAR
This menu will serve 25.

Prepare this sampler of desserts for a holiday gathering, and be prepared for star status. Sweets are as much a part of the Christmas season as Santa Claus himself, especially when they're the focal point of a Christmas get-together. Chocolates and fruits, punches and coffees—something for everyone is included in this list of luscious treats.

WHITE FUDGE TERRINE

1¾ cups chopped almonds, toasted and divided
¾ pound white chocolate, finely chopped
⅔ cup whipping cream
¾ cup chopped glacéed apricots
¼ cup finely chopped dates
2 tablespoons port or other sweet red wine
½ teaspoon vanilla extract
Sliced almonds, toasted
Additional glacéed apricots

Sprinkle ¼ cup chopped almonds in the bottom of a lightly greased 7½- x 3- x 2-inch loafpan; set aside.

Place white chocolate in top of a double boiler; place over simmering water, and immediately remove double boiler from heat. Let stand, without stirring, while heating cream. Bring cream almost to a boil in a small saucepan over medium heat. Pour cream over chocolate, stirring until chocolate melts and mixture is smooth. Add apricots, dates, port, vanilla, and 1¼ cups chopped almonds, mixing well.

Spoon chocolate mixture into prepared loafpan, pressing down and smoothing surface. Sprinkle remaining ¼ cup chopped almonds over top, and press lightly into chocolate mixture. Cover and chill overnight.

To unmold, dip in hot water about 30 seconds. Invert onto serving platter, and tap gently to release.

Left: Crispy Meringue Sticks dipped in cool Gingered Chocolate offer an unusual way to tempt the palate. Delicate and rich at the same time, they offer the extra advantage of being a prepare-ahead dish.

Opposite: Build a fire, place sheet music for Christmas carols on the piano, and lay out this lovely selection to create an evening to remember. Clockwise from right: Meringue Sticks with Gingered Chocolate, Old-Fashioned Fruit Torte, Sparkling Punch, and Blue Cheese Spread with Almond Rusks and apple wedges.

Garnish with sliced almonds and apricots. Let stand at room temperature for 10 minutes before slicing. Yield: 12 servings.

Microwave Conversion:
Prepare loafpan as directed above.
Place white chocolate in a large glass bowl; microwave at MEDIUM (50% power) for 5 to 6 minutes, stirring every 2 minutes, until chocolate melts. Place cream in a 1-cup glass measuring cup, and microwave at HIGH for 1 to 1½ minutes or until hot. Gently pour hot cream over chocolate, stirring constantly until smooth. Proceed as instructed above.

MERINGUE STICKS WITH GINGERED CHOCOLATE CREAM
½ cup sifted powdered sugar
½ cup superfine sugar
2 tablespoons cocoa
3 egg whites
¼ teaspoon cream of tartar
Sifted cocoa
Additional sifted powdered sugar
Gingered Chocolate Cream (recipe follows)

Line a large greased baking sheet with parchment paper; set aside.
Sift together first 3 ingredients. Beat egg whites (at room temperature) and cream of tartar in a medium mixing bowl until soft peaks form. Add sugar mixture, 1 tablespoon at a time, beating until stiff peaks form. Spoon meringue mixture into a pastry bag fitted with a ½-inch plain tip.
Pipe meringue mixture into 16-inch lengths about ½-inch apart on prepared baking sheet. Bake at 200° for 1 hour. Turn oven off, and allow Meringue Sticks to cool in oven 2 hours. (Do not open oven door.)
Carefully remove Meringue Sticks from parchment paper. Cut or snap Meringue Sticks into approximately 4-inch lengths. Dip ends of each Meringue Stick in cocoa or powdered sugar. Store in airtight containers.
Serve Gingered Chocolate Cream in a

chilled serving bowl with Meringue Sticks for dipping. Yield: about 4½ dozen (4-inch) sticks.

Gingered Chocolate Cream:
1 cup whipping cream
4 (1-ounce) squares semisweet chocolate, chopped
3 tablespoons minced crystallized ginger

Combine cream and chocolate in a small saucepan; cook, stirring occasionally, over medium heat until chocolate melts. Pour chocolate mixture into a medium glass bowl; cover and refrigerate 1½ hours or until mixture is slightly chilled. (If mixture gets too cold, it will become too firm to beat until fluffy. Let stand at room temperature until soft enough to beat.)
Beat mixture at medium speed of an electric mixer until thick and fluffy. Gently fold in ginger. Cover with plastic wrap, and chill until serving time. Yield: about 1¾ cups.

PRALINE LAYER CAKE
⅔ cup butter or margarine, softened
1½ cups sugar
2 eggs
1¾ cups all-purpose flour
⅔ cup cocoa
¾ teaspoon soda
¼ teaspoon baking powder
⅛ teaspoon salt
⅔ cup milk
1 teaspoon vanilla extract
⅓ cup praline liqueur
Caramel Filling (recipe follows)
Chocolate Butter Frosting (recipe follows)
Pecan halves, toasted

Grease and flour a 15- x 10- x 1-inch jellyroll pan; set aside.
Cream butter in a large mixing bowl; gradually add sugar, beating well. Add eggs, one at a time, beating well after each addition.
Combine next 5 ingredients; add to creamed mixture alternately with milk, beginning and ending with flour mixture. Stir in

vanilla. Pour batter into prepared pan, smoothing evenly with a spatula.

Bake at 350° for 18 minutes or until a wooden pick inserted in center comes out clean. Cool cake in pan 5 minutes; loosen cake from sides of pan, and turn out onto a large towel. Transfer cake to a rack, using towel to lift it, and cool completely.

Sprinkle praline liqueur evenly over surface of cake. Cut cake into three 10- x 5-inch rectangles, using a long serrated knife. Measure out and reserve ¼ cup Caramel Filling. Assemble rectangles on top of each other on cake plate, spreading Caramel Filling between layers, and Chocolate Butter Frosting on top and sides of cake. Garnish with toasted pecans, and drizzle with reserved ¼ cup Caramel Filling. Yield: 10 servings.

Caramel Filling:
1¼ cups sugar
¼ teaspoon salt
¼ teaspoon cream of tartar
¼ cup plus 1 tablespoon water
¼ cup plus 2 tablespoons whipping cream
½ cup butter, cut into ½-inch pieces

Combine first 4 ingredients in a small saucepan. Bring to a boil, stirring constantly; cook, without stirring, over medium-high heat until candy thermometer registers 342°.

Remove from heat, and add cream and butter (do not stir). Let stand until butter melts. Stir caramel mixture gently with a wire whisk until well blended; transfer to a small bowl, and let stand until room temperature. Yield: enough filling for one layer cake.

Chocolate Butter Frosting:
½ cup butter, softened
3 cups sifted powdered sugar
3 (1-ounce) squares unsweetened chocolate, melted and cooled
3 tablespoons milk
1 teaspoon vanilla extract

Cream butter; gradually add sugar, beating well. Gradually add remaining ingredients; beat until light and fluffy. Yield: enough for one 3-layer cake.

OLD-FASHIONED FRUIT TORTE
Flaky Pastry (recipe follows)
½ cup sugar
1½ tablespoons all-purpose flour
Dash of salt
2 egg yolks
1½ cups milk
½ teaspoon vanilla extract
2 (10-ounce) jars raspberry preserves
¼ cup brandy or fruit-flavored liqueur
Sifted powdered sugar
Chocolate curls

Prepare pastry, and chill at least 1 hour.

Divide pastry into 12 equal portions. Roll out 1 portion of dough on back of a lightly floured 8-inch cakepan, and trim around edge to form a circle (dough will be very thin); prick pastry with a fork.

Bake pastry on cakepan at 450° for 6 to 8 minutes or until lightly browned. Carefully transfer pastry to a cooling rack; repeat rolling and baking procedure, using remaining dough to make 12 pastry circles. Set pastry circles aside.

Combine sugar, flour, and salt in a small heavy saucepan. Beat egg yolks in a small mixing bowl; add milk, mixing well. Stir into dry ingredients; cook over medium heat, stirring constantly, until mixture is smooth and thick. Remove from heat and stir in vanilla. Cool custard completely.

Combine raspberry preserves and brandy, stirring well. Spread raspberry mixture evenly on 6 pastry layers. Spread cooled custard evenly over remaining 6 layers. Stack custard and raspberry layers alternately, beginning with a custard layer and ending with a raspberry layer. Cover loosely with plastic wrap, and refrigerate overnight.

Sprinkle powdered sugar around top edge of torte, and garnish with chocolate curls. Let stand at room temperature 30 minutes before slicing into thin wedges. Yield: 12 servings.

Flaky Pastry:
3 cups all-purpose flour
1½ teaspoons salt
1 cup plus 2 tablespoons shortening
¼ cup plus 3 tablespoons cold water

Combine flour and salt in a medium bowl; cut in shortening with a pastry blender until mixture resembles coarse meal. Sprinkle cold water evenly over surface; stir with a fork to moisten dry ingredients. Shape into a ball; chill. Yield: enough pastry to make 13 thin pastry circles or one 9-inch double-crust pie.

SPECIAL PINEAPPLE CHEESECAKE
1 (15¼-ounce) can crushed pineapple, undrained
3 (8-ounce) packages cream cheese, softened
1 cup sugar, divided
5 eggs
1 (8-ounce) carton sour cream
½ teaspoon vanilla extract
Walnut Crust (recipe follows)
1 tablespoon cornstarch
1 cup fresh or frozen thawed cranberries
Walnut halves
Candied kumquats (optional)

Drain pineapple, reserving juice. Set aside.
Beat cream cheese in a large mixing bowl until light and fluffy; gradually add ⅔ cup sugar, mixing well. Add eggs, one at a time, beating at low speed of electric mixer until well blended. Stir in sour cream, vanilla, and crushed pineapple.
Pour mixture into Walnut Crust. Bake at 350° for 45 minutes; reduce temperature to 225°, and bake an additional 30 minutes or

Opposite: Guests become involved in the entertaining process when you arrange a lavish Coffee Bar, such as the one presented here. Chocolate chips, whipped cream, and brown and white sugars combine with various liqueurs for an array of tantalizing choices. Include the Special Pineapple Cheesecake shown in the foreground, and you have the recipe for a surefire dessert party success.

until set. Cool completely on a wire rack.
Combine remaining ⅓ cup sugar and cornstarch in a small saucepan; stir well. Add water to reserved pineapple juice to measure ⅔ cup. Add juice mixture and cranberries to saucepan; cook over high heat 1 minute. Reduce heat, and simmer, stirring frequently, 8 to 12 minutes or until cranberries pop and mixture is thickened and bubbly. Cool to room temperature. Spoon cranberry mixture evenly over cheesecake; cover with plastic wrap and refrigerate cheesecake overnight.
Remove side of springform pan; transfer cheesecake to a serving platter. Garnish with walnut halves and kumquats, if desired. Yield: 16 servings.

Walnut Crust:
1 cup graham cracker crumbs
½ cup chopped walnuts, toasted
¼ cup firmly packed brown sugar
¼ cup butter or margarine, melted

Combine first 3 ingredients, mixing well. Stir in butter; press mixture firmly in bottom of a 9-inch springform pan. Bake at 375° for 8 to 10 minutes. Cool completely on a wire rack. Yield: one 9-inch crust.

CHERRY FRUITCAKES
5 (1⁵⁄₁₆-ounce) white chocolate candy bars with almonds, coarsely broken
1 cup coarsely chopped candied red cherries
2 cups all-purpose flour, divided
2 cups mashed ripe bananas (about 4 large bananas)
½ cup vegetable oil
½ cup sugar
3 eggs, beaten
1 teaspoon vanilla extract
1 teaspoon soda
½ teaspoon baking powder
¼ teaspoon salt
Candied red or green cherries

Combine white chocolate and chopped

cherries in a large bowl; sprinkle with ⅓ cup flour. Toss well, and set aside.

Combine bananas, oil, sugar, eggs, and vanilla in a large bowl, stirring until the mixture is well blended. Combine the remaining 1⅔ cups flour, soda, baking powder, and salt in a medium bowl; gradually add this to the banana mixture, blending well. Gently fold in the reserved white chocolate mixture. Spoon the batter into 2 well-greased 8½- x 4½- x 3-inch loafpans.

Bake at 350° for 55 minutes or until a wooden pick inserted in center comes out clean. Cool in pans 10 minutes; remove from pans, and cool completely on a wire rack. Garnish each loaf with candied cherries, if desired. Yield: 2 loaves.

BLUE CHEESE SPREAD WITH ALMOND RUSKS
2 (4-ounce) packages blue cheese, crumbled
1 (8-ounce) package cream cheese, softened
½ cup butter or margarine, softened
3 tablespoons minced onion
Almond Rusks (recipe follows)
Green and red apple wedges

Combine first 4 ingredients in a medium mixing bowl; beat on high speed of electric mixer until well blended. Mound cheese mixture onto a serving platter, smoothing the sides with a spatula. Cover cheese mixture and chill overnight.

Let cheese stand at room temperature 15 minutes; surround cheese spread with Almond Rusks and apple wedges. Yield: 12 appetizer servings.

Almond Rusks:
1¾ cups all-purpose flour
¾ cup finely chopped almonds, toasted
1 teaspoon baking powder
¼ teaspoon salt
¼ cup half-and-half
1 egg, lightly beaten
Melted butter or margarine

Combine first 4 ingredients in a large mixing bowl; stir well. Combine half-and-half and egg; add to flour mixture. Stir with a wooden spoon until well blended. (Dough will be very stiff.)

Turn dough out onto a lightly floured surface; form into a 12-inch log, dusting dough with flour as necessary. Transfer log to a greased and floured baking sheet. Bake at 350° for 35 minutes; cool on a wire rack 20 minutes.

Carefully slip a spatula under roll to loosen. Cut into ½-inch slices with an electric or serrated knife, and arrange on a baking sheet. Lightly brush each rusk with melted butter; bake at 350° for 20 minutes or until crisp. Cool and store in an airtight container. Yield: 2 dozen.

SPARKLING PUNCH
1 cup superfine sugar
¾ cup freshly squeezed lemon juice, chilled
2½ cups light rum, chilled
1 (750-ml) bottle champagne, chilled

Combine sugar and lemon juice in a punch bowl, stirring until sugar dissolves. Stir in rum; add champagne just before serving. Serve immediately over crushed ice, if desired. Yield: 8 cups.

COFFEE BAR
10 cups hot coffee
1 cup sugar cubes
1 cup brown sugar
1 (6-ounce) package miniature semisweet chocolate morsels
1 cup whipping cream, whipped
Assorted liqueurs and spirits: Amaretto, Kahlua or coffee liqueur, brandy, crème de cacao, crème de menthe, bourbon, etc.

Serve all ingredients buffet-style, letting each guest create his own dessert coffee. Yield: 10 servings.

CHRISTMAS MORNING DELIGHTS

If visions of sugarplums danced in their heads all night, Christmas morning breakfast will be a welcome sight. Whether it's a quick pick-me-up before the presents, or a lazy, joyful feast afterward, delight your Christmas revelers with choices from this assortment of breakfast and brunch delicacies.

PEAR BUNDLES
¼ cup brandy or crème de cassis
¼ cup seedless raisins
2 tablespoons chopped pecans
2 tablespoons brown sugar
4 small fresh pears
2 tablespoons lemon juice
½ (17¼-ounce) package frozen puff pastry (1 sheet)
¾ cup whipping cream

Combine first 4 ingredients in a small mixing bowl, stirring well; cover and let stand at room temperature overnight.

Drain raisin mixture, reserving liquid. Peel pears, removing core and stem, but leaving whole pears intact. Brush surface of each pear with lemon juice, and fill center with raisin mixture. Set aside.

Thaw puff pastry according to package directions, and unfold on a lightly floured surface. Cut pastry sheet (lengthwise, then crosswise) into 4 equal portions; roll each portion into an 8-inch square. Place one pear, stem side up, in center of one pastry square. Lightly brush edges of square with water; bring edges of pastry up to stem end, pressing pastry to surface of pear. Gently press pastry together at stem end to seal, and trim away excess pastry. Cut "leaves" from excess pastry; brush with water, and attach to the stem end, pressing gently to adhere.

Right: Here are some ways to offer glad tidings and good health on Christmas morning. Clockwise from bottom: Broiled Grapefruit Compotes, Pear Bundles, and Healthy Orange Granola.

Repeat procedure with remaining pastry squares and pears.

Place pears on a lightly greased baking sheet. Bake at 425° for 25 minutes or until golden brown.

Combine reserved liquid with whipping cream, stirring well. Serve pears warm with cream mixture. Yield: 4 servings.

BROILED GRAPEFRUIT COMPOTE
1 (12-ounce) package pitted dried prunes
1 cup water
2 tablespoons brown sugar
2 tablespoons butter or margarine
¼ teaspoon mace
3 large pink grapefruit, halved

Combine prunes and water in a small saucepan; bring to a boil. Cover, reduce heat, and simmer 10 minutes. Remove prunes using a slotted spoon, and set aside. Bring prune liquid to a boil; boil over high heat, until liquid reduces to 2 tablespoons. Remove from heat, and add sugar, butter, and mace, stirring until butter melts.

Remove seeds, and loosen sections of each grapefruit half, using a small sharp knife. Remove every other grapefruit section, and reserve for other uses. Place 1 prune in each empty grapefruit section. Brush top of each grapefruit half with sugar mixture, and place on rack in a broiler pan. Broil 6 inches from heat source for 2 minutes or until surface is glazed and grapefruit is hot. Serve immediately. Yield: 6 servings.

HEALTHY ORANGE GRANOLA
2 cups regular oats, uncooked
1 cup flaked coconut
½ cup coarsely chopped pecans or walnuts
½ cup unsalted sunflower kernels
½ cup bran cereal
½ cup honey
⅓ cup vegetable oil
Grated rind of 1 orange
1½ cups dried fruit bits

Combine first 5 ingredients in a lightly greased 13- x 9- x 2-inch baking dish; mix well. Combine honey, vegetable oil, and orange rind. Pour over oats mixture, stirring until well combined.

Bake at 300° for 40 minutes, stirring every 10 minutes. Add dried fruit bits, stirring well. Cool completely. Stir frequently during cooling to prevent lumping. Store in airtight containers. Yield: about 6 cups.

Microwave Conversion:
Combine ingredients as directed above in a 12- x 8- x 2-inch glass baking dish. Microwave uncovered at HIGH for 8 minutes, stirring every 2 minutes. Proceed as directed above.

INDIVIDUAL BRUNCH STRUDELS
½ cup plus 2 tablespoons butter or margarine, divided
2 tablespoons all-purpose flour
1 cup milk
¼ cup freshly grated Parmesan cheese
Dash of red pepper
1 tablespoon minced fresh parsley
1 tablespoon minced onion
5 eggs, beaten
½ pound crabmeat, rinsed and drained
6 sheets frozen phyllo pastry, thawed
¼ cup fine dry breadcrumbs
Phyllo Bows (recipe follows)

Melt 2 tablespoons butter in a small saucepan over low heat; add flour, stirring until smooth. Gradually add milk; cook over medium heat, stirring constantly, until thickened and bubbly. Remove from heat, and stir in cheese and red pepper. Set aside.

Melt 2 tablespoons butter in a large skillet over low heat; add parsley and onion; sauté until tender. Stir in eggs; cook over low heat, stirring often, until eggs are firm but still moist (do not overcook). Remove from heat; stir in cheese sauce. Cool completely. Stir in crabmeat; set aside.

Melt remaining ¼ cup plus 2 tablespoons butter in a small saucepan. Place one sheet phyllo on a dry surface; brush lightly with one-sixth of butter, and sprinkle with one-sixth of breadcrumbs. (Cover remaining phyllo pastry sheets with a damp towel to prevent drying.) Fold in half lengthwise; spread about ½ cup crab mixture in a 3-inch strip down center of pastry, starting from a short end. Fold outer edges of pastry over filling, and carefully fold pastry, end over end (filled end first), down the entire length of pastry. Cover with a damp towel, and set aside. Repeat procedure with remaining butter, pastry sheets, breadcrumbs, and crab mixture to make 6 bundles.

Place strudels, seam sides down, on a lightly greased baking sheet. Cover with plastic wrap, and refrigerate several hours or overnight until ready to bake.

Remove plastic wrap, and bake at 350° for 15 minutes or until lightly brown. Cool 5 minutes; transfer to individual serving plates. Gently place a Phyllo Bow on each pastry. Yield: 6 servings.

Phyllo Bows:
6 sheets frozen phyllo pastry, thawed
Melted butter or margarine

Place one sheet phyllo on a dry surface; brush lightly with butter. Cut a ½-inch lengthwise strip from pastry; set strip aside. Fold one short end of sheet in 1½ inches. Continue folding, over and over, to opposite edge, forming a 1½-inch-wide strip. Fold under each end of strip to make a 3½-inch-long strip. Lightly pinch middle in; wrap reserved ½-inch-wide length around middle to form a bow. Repeat process with butter and remaining sheets of phyllo.

Arrange bows in a lightly greased jellyroll pan. Bake at 350° for 15 minutes or until lightly browned. Cool completely. Yield: 6 bows.

Below: Topped with festive pastry bows, Individual Brunch Strudels contain a tasty crabmeat mixture.

BRANDIED APPLE RINGS
WITH LEMON TOPPING

3 tablespoons butter or margarine, melted
2 tablespoons brown sugar
2 tablespoons brandy or applejack
1 teaspoon ground cinnamon
4 medium-size baking apples, unpeeled
2 tablespoons lemon juice
¾ cup chopped dates
Lemon Topping (recipe follows)

Combine first 4 ingredients in a 1-cup glass measure; stir well, and set aside.

Remove apple cores and stems, leaving apples intact; cut into ½-inch-thick rings. Sprinkle rings on both sides with lemon juice. Layer apple rings in a lightly greased 13- x 9- x 2-inch baking dish. Place dates in centers of apple rings. Drizzle reserved butter mixture over all.

Cover and bake at 375° for 35 minutes or until tender. Remove from oven, and cool 10 minutes. Serve apples warm with Lemon Topping. Yield: 6 to 8 servings.

Microwave Conversion:

Assemble the apples and dates, as directed above, in a lightly greased 12- x 8- x 2-inch glass baking dish. Drizzle the reserved butter mixture over all.

Cover with heavy-duty plastic wrap, and microwave at HIGH for 6 to 7 minutes, turning after 3 minutes. Let stand 2 minutes, and serve warm with Lemon Topping.

Lemon Topping:

2½ tablespoons sugar
½ tablespoon all-purpose flour
½ teaspoon grated lemon rind
2 tablespoons lemon juice
1 egg, lightly beaten
½ cup miniature marshmallows
½ cup vanilla-flavored yogurt

Combine sugar and flour in a small non-aluminum saucepan; add next 3 ingredients, stirring until flour dissolves. Stir in marshmallows. Cook, stirring frequently, over medium heat until marshmallows melt and mixture

thickens. Remove mixture from heat, and cool completely.

Fold in yogurt. Cover with plastic wrap, and chill thoroughly. Yield: 1 cup.

Microwave Conversion:

Combine sugar and flour in a small glass bowl; add next 3 ingredients, stirring until flour dissolves. Stir in marshmallows. Cover with heavy-duty plastic wrap, and microwave at HIGH for 2 to 2½ minutes, stirring every 30 seconds until marshmallows melt and mixture thickens. Remove from heat, and cool completely. Proceed as directed above.

BACON AND POTATO PUFF OMELET

2 tablespoons butter or margarine
3 (¼-inch-thick) slices Canadian bacon, cut into thin strips
¼ pound new potatoes, unpeeled and thinly sliced
6 eggs, separated
½ teaspoon dried dillweed
¼ teaspoon salt
½ cup (2 ounces) shredded Monterey Jack cheese

Melt butter in a heavy, 10-inch skillet over medium heat; add bacon, and sauté until barely cooked. Remove bacon, using a slotted spoon, and drain on paper towels, reserving drippings in skillet. Add potatoes to skillet and cook over medium heat until tender, turning frequently. Remove potatoes, using a slotted spoon, and drain on paper towels. Set aside.

Beat egg whites (at room temperature) in a large mixing bowl until stiff but not dry; set aside.

Beat egg yolks in a small mixing bowl at high speed of an electric mixer until thick and pale (about 5 minutes). Stir in dillweed and salt. Fold the yolk mixture into the egg whites.

Pour egg mixture into skillet, and gently smooth surface, using a spatula. Cook over medium-low heat 5 minutes; remove from heat, and arrange cooked potatoes over top. Arrange bacon strips over potatoes. Cook 5 additional minutes. Remove from heat, and sprinkle with cheese.

Broil 6 inches from heat source 1 minute or until cheese melts. Cut omelet into wedges, and serve immediately from skillet. Yield: 8 servings.

CRISP BELGIAN WAFFLES

1½ cups milk
¼ cup butter or margarine, melted
2 eggs
2 cups all-purpose flour
2 tablespoons sugar
1 tablespoon baking powder
1 teaspoon salt
Easy Praline Sauce (recipe follows)
Assorted toppings: sifted powdered
    sugar, fresh fruit, flavored yogurt,
    toasted coconut, chocolate curls, sour
    cream, or crème fraîche

Combine first 3 ingredients in an electric blender container; process until smooth. Add flour, sugar, baking powder, and salt; process until smooth, scraping sides of blender container as necessary.

Cook batter on a preheated, lightly oiled waffle iron, according to manufacturer's directions. Remove cooked waffles, and keep warm while preparing remaining waffles. Serve Belgian Waffles hot with Easy Praline Sauce and a choice of toppings. Yield: twelve 3-inch waffles.

Easy Praline Sauce:
⅓ cup butter or margarine
1 cup chopped pecans
1 cup maple syrup

Melt butter in a small skillet over low heat; add pecans. Cook, stirring frequently, about 5 minutes or until pecans are toasted. Add maple syrup, stirring well. Cook until thoroughly heated.

Serve warm with waffles, pancakes, or French toast. Yield: 1½ cups.

HONEY BLINTZES

2 (3-ounce) packages cream cheese,
    softened
2 tablespoons powdered sugar
1 tablespoon honey
1 tablespoon plain yogurt or
    sour cream
1 tablespoon amaretto
1 (8-ounce) can refrigerator crescent
    dinner rolls
Apple Cinnamon Sauce
    (recipe follows)
1 medium apple, thinly sliced

Beat cream cheese in a small mixing bowl until creamy. Add next 4 ingredients, beating until smooth. Unroll dinner rolls, and separate into triangles. Gently press each triangle on a lightly floured surface until it is ½ inch larger than its original size, and all sides of triangle are equal in length.

Spread about 2 tablespoons cream cheese mixture over surface of triangle, to within ¼ inch of each edge. Starting at one side of each triangle, roll up jellyroll fashion halfway toward opposite point. Fold 2 side points in toward center, and continue to roll up jellyroll fashion toward remaining point. Moisten and pinch all edges to seal. Repeat procedure, using remaining dinner rolls and cream cheese mixture.

Carefully transfer blintzes to lightly greased baking sheets. Bake at 375° for 8 minutes or until golden brown. Serve Honey Blintzes warm with Apple Cinnamon Sauce, and garnish each serving with fresh apple slices. Yield: 8 servings.

Apple Cinnamon Sauce:
1 (8-ounce) carton vanilla-flavored
    yogurt
¼ cup applesauce
¼ teaspoon ground cinnamon
Dash of ground nutmeg

Combine all ingredients in a small bowl, stirring until smooth. Serve Apple Cinnamon Sauce with blintzes, waffles, or pancakes. Yield: about 1 cup.

COME FOR DRINKS AND NIBBLES

HOT SPIKED KABOBS
ASPARAGUS-CHICKEN APPETIZER BARS
PIMIENTO DIP WITH FRESH VEGETABLES
SOFT PRETZELS WITH OLIVE-WALNUT DIP
MARINATED CHEESE
HERBED SHORTBREAD WITH
MUSTARD CHUTNEY AND ASSORTED CHEESES
TOFFEE SQUARES
HOT TEA TODDY
CRANBERRY CHILLER
COFFEE EGGNOG
This menu serves 25.

For gala parties, encourage a lively atmosphere by serving drinks and nibbles. Offer enticing appetizers and beverages throughout your entertaining area. This will coax your company to mix and mingle as they find their way to mouth-watering sensations, and get to know each other as they go.

HOT SPIKED KABOBS
4 pounds boneless chicken breasts (skin removed) cut into 1-inch pieces
2 cups commercial chili sauce
1⅓ cups Kahlua or other coffee-flavored liqueur
½ cup minced onion
2 (8-ounce) cans pineapple chunks, drained
2 medium-size green or red bell peppers, seeded and cut into 1-inch squares

Place chicken in a shallow container. Combine chili sauce, liqueur, and onion in a small bowl, mixing well. Pour over chicken.

Right: Foster a friendly flow of party guests by positioning appetizing dishes in select spots around the room. Front to back: Pimiento Dip with fresh vegetables, Hot Spiked Kabobs, Marinated Cheese, Cranberry Chiller, and Soft Pretzels with Olive-Walnut Dip.

114

Cover chicken with plastic wrap, and refrigerate overnight.

Remove chicken from marinade, reserving marinade. Alternate chicken, pineapple chunks, and pepper squares on twelve 6-inch bamboo skewers. Arrange on lightly greased rack of a roasting pan.

Broil 6 inches from heat for 4 to 5 minutes on each side, basting often with marinade. Serve hot. Yield: 12 appetizers.

ASPARAGUS-CHICKEN APPETIZER BARS

4 boneless chicken breast halves, cooked, and cut into 1-inch pieces
1 cup soft breadcrumbs
¼ cup sour cream
½ teaspoon salt
¼ teaspoon red pepper
½ (17¼-ounce) package frozen puff pastry (1 sheet), thawed
2 (8-ounce) packages frozen asparagus spears, thawed and patted dry
¼ cup grated Parmesan cheese, divided

Combine first 5 ingredients in a food processor bowl fitted with steel chopping blade. Process 3 to 5 seconds or until well blended.

Unfold pastry; cut in half crosswise. Roll one half on a lightly floured surface to a 14- x 10-inch rectangle. Place rectangle on a large ungreased baking sheet. Place half of the asparagus spears in a row along one long side of pastry (about 1 inch apart), arranging cut ends of asparagus in center of pastry with tips extending just to edge. Spoon half of chicken mixture over asparagus spears, spreading with spoon to within 1 inch of tips. Fold pastry over, covering chicken mixture and leaving 1 inch of asparagus exposed. Gently seal sides; sprinkle pastry with 2 tablespoons Parmesan cheese. Repeat procedure on another baking sheet, using remaining pastry, asparagus, chicken mixture, and cheese.

Bake at 375° for 25 minutes or until puffed and golden brown. Cut between asparagus spears into bars, and serve immediately. Yield: about 2 dozen.

PIMIENTO DIP

1 (4-ounce) jar whole pimientos, drained and patted dry
1 large ripe tomato, peeled, quartered, and seeded
1 clove garlic
¼ cup mayonnaise
1 tablespoon red wine vinegar
⅛ teaspoon salt
⅛ teaspoon freshly ground pepper
⅛ teaspoon red pepper
¼ cup olive oil
Chopped chives

Combine first 8 ingredients in an electric blender container; process until smooth. With blender running, gradually add oil in a slow, steady stream until incorporated. Process 30 additional seconds.

Transfer mixture to a bowl; cover and refrigerate overnight.

Garnish dip with chives, and serve with fresh vegetables. Yield: 1¾ cups.

SOFT PRETZELS WITH OLIVE-WALNUT DIP

2 packages dry yeast
3 tablespoons sugar
2 cups warm water (105° to 115°)
2 egg yolks, beaten
2 tablespoons butter or margarine, melted
2 teaspoons salt
5 cups unbleached flour, divided
1 egg
1 tablespoon water
About ¼ cup coarse salt
Olive-Walnut Dip (recipe follows)

Dissolve yeast and sugar in warm water in a large mixing bowl; let stand 5 minutes or until bubbly. Add egg yolks, butter, salt, and half of flour, stirring until blended. Add enough flour to make a soft dough.

Turn dough out onto a lightly floured surface, and knead 5 minutes or until smooth and elastic. Place dough in a greased bowl, turning to grease top. Cover and let rise in a warm place (85°), free from drafts, 30 minutes or until doubled in bulk.

Divide dough into 48 equal portions; roll each into a 14-inch rope. Shape into pretzels, and place on greased baking sheets.

Combine egg and 1 tablespoon water, stirring with a fork until well blended. Brush pretzels lightly with egg mixture; sprinkle lightly with coarse salt. Bake at 375° for 12 minutes or until golden brown. Transfer to wire racks, and cool completely. Serve with Olive-Walnut Dip. Yield: 4 dozen.

Olive-Walnut Dip:
1 (8-ounce) package cream cheese, softened
¼ cup butter or margarine, softened
½ cup finely chopped walnuts
½ cup sour cream
⅓ cup chopped pimiento-stuffed olives
2 tablespoons sherry
1 clove garlic, minced
Walnut halves
Sliced pimiento-stuffed olives

Beat cream cheese and butter in a medium mixing bowl until fluffy; add next 5 ingredients, stirring until smooth. Cover and refrigerate overnight.

Spoon chilled dip into a serving bowl, and garnish with walnut halves and sliced olives. Serve with Soft Pretzels. Yield: about 2 cups.

MARINATED CHEESE
½ cup olive oil
½ cup white wine vinegar
¼ cup chopped fresh parsley or cilantro
2 tablespoons minced green onion
2 cloves garlic, minced
1 teaspoon sugar
½ teaspoon salt
½ teaspoon dried basil leaves
½ teaspoon freshly ground pepper
1 (8-ounce) package cream cheese, chilled
½ pound (5½- x 2- x 1-inch) block sharp Cheddar cheese, chilled

Combine first 9 ingredients in a small jar; cover tightly, and shake vigorously to blend. Set aside.

Cut cream cheese crosswise into ¼-inch strips. Cut each strip in half to form 2 squares. Set aside. Cut Cheddar cheese in same manner.

Layer cheese slices in a shallow container, alternating cream cheese and Cheddar side by side, and standing them up on edge. Pour marinade over cheese. Cover and refrigerate overnight. Drain and arrange on a platter in same layered fashion. Serve with crackers. Yield: 16 appetizer servings.

HERBED SHORTBREAD
1½ cups all-purpose flour
1 cup regular oats, uncooked
1 cup (4 ounces) shredded Gruyére cheese
½ cup butter, chilled and cut into ½-inch pieces
⅓ cup dried parsley flakes
1 egg
1 teaspoon freshly ground pepper
Assorted cheeses
Spicy Mustard Chutney (recipe follows)

Combine first 7 ingredients in a food processor bowl fitted with steel chopping blade; process until dough forms a ball. Shape dough into a cylinder 1½ inches in diameter. Wrap in plastic wrap, and chill.

Cut dough cylinder into ¼-inch slices; place slices on an ungreased baking sheet. Bake at 350° for 25 minutes or until lightly browned; remove from baking sheet, and cool completely on wire racks.

Serve with assorted cheeses and Spicy Mustard Chutney. Yield: 2½ dozen.

Spicy Mustard Chutney:
1 (9-ounce) jar chutney
2 tablespoons dry mustard
2 tablespoons white wine vinegar
½ teaspoon freshly ground pepper
¼ teaspoon dried basil leaves

Combine all ingredients in a small bowl; stir well. Cover and chill thoroughly. Yield: about 1 cup.

TOFFEE SQUARES

½ cup butter, softened
½ cup plus 3 tablespoons sugar, divided
½ teaspoon vanilla extract
1 cup plus 1½ tablespoons all-purpose
  flour, divided
1 (2.2-ounce) package slivered almonds,
  toasted and coarsely chopped
1½ tablespoons whipping cream
2 tablespoons butter
4 (1-ounce) squares semisweet chocolate,
  coarsely chopped
1 tablespoon shortening

Cream ½ cup butter in a medium mixing bowl; gradually add ½ cup sugar, beating until light and fluffy. Stir in vanilla. Add 1 cup flour; stir until blended. With floured hands, press into an ungreased 9-inch square baking pan. Bake at 350° for 20 minutes; set aside on wire rack.

Combine almonds, remaining 3 tablespoons sugar, and 1½ tablespoons flour in a small saucepan, mixing well. Stir in cream and butter. Cook, stirring constantly, over medium heat until sugar dissolves and butter melts. Pour immediately over crust.

Bake at 350° for 15 to 20 minutes or until golden brown. Cool in pan 10 minutes on wire rack. Loosen edges; cut into 1½-inch squares. Cool completely on wire racks.

Combine chocolate and shortening in top of a double boiler; place over simmering water. Cook just until chocolate and shortening melt, stirring gently until well blended. Remove from heat, and cool slightly.

Dip half of each square in melted chocolate, and transfer to wire rack. Let stand until chocolate is firm. Yield: 3 dozen.

HOT TEA TODDY

1 quart water
2 quarts apple cider
3 (3-inch) sticks cinnamon
2 quart-size tea bags
3 cups brandy

Combine first 3 ingredients in a large

Dutch oven; bring to a boil. Add tea bags, remove from heat, and cover. Let stand 10 minutes. Remove tea bags, and stir in brandy. Serve hot. Yield: 15 cups.

CRANBERRY CHILLER

3 cups fresh or frozen, thawed
  cranberries
1 cup orange juice
½ cup sugar
2 (32-ounce) jars cranberry juice cocktail,
  chilled
1 (750-ml) bottle rum, chilled
1 (12-ounce) can frozen lemonade
  concentrate, thawed
1 (32-ounce) bottle ginger ale, chilled

Combine cranberries, orange juice, and sugar in saucepan, stirring well. Bring to a boil; reduce heat, and simmer 7 minutes. Pour into 3½-cup ring mold; cool to room temperature. Cover and freeze overnight.

Combine cranberry juice cocktail, rum, and lemonade concentrate in a large punch bowl, stirring gently. Unmold ice ring into punch just before serving; add ginger ale, stirring gently. Yield: about 16 cups.

COFFEE EGGNOG

4 eggs
¼ cup plus 1 tablespoon sugar
1 cup half-and-half
1½ cups strong brewed coffee, chilled
¼ cup brandy
¼ cup rum
¼ cup Kahlua or other coffee-flavored
  liqueur
1 cup whipping cream
Ground nutmeg

Beat eggs in a large mixing bowl until thick and pale (about 5 minutes); gradually add sugar, beating well. Beat in next 5 ingredients. Cover and chill at least 2 hours.

Beat whipping cream until soft peaks form. Fold into egg mixture. Serve in punch cups; sprinkle with nutmeg. Yield: 7 cups.

SAVE TIME WITH MAKE-AHEAD MEALS

Whether you'll be creating an intimate family dinner or feeding friendly throngs, planning ahead for holiday meals will allow you to enjoy the festivities, too. These recipes provide main dishes, breads, even salads and appetizers, which can be prepared early and frozen, and then served when needed during the bustling Christmas season. Some recipes include microwave conversions.

FROSTY TOMATO SALAD

1 (28-ounce) can whole tomatoes, drained
1 cup tomato and chile cocktail juice
¼ cup minced onion
1 teaspoon dried basil leaves
¼ teaspoon celery seeds
⅛ teaspoon red pepper
Dash of salt
Lettuce leaves
Avocado slices
Lemon slices

Combine tomatoes, cocktail juice, onion, basil, celery seeds, red pepper, and salt in an electric blender container. Cover and process 20 seconds.

Pour mixture into an 8-inch square baking pan. Cover and freeze 4 hours, stirring every hour.

Shape tomato mixture into balls, using an ice cream scoop; place on a baking sheet, and freeze until firm. Place frozen balls in heavy-duty zip-top plastic bags or freezer container; seal, label, and freeze up to 1 month.

Serve frozen tomato mixture on a lettuce-lined serving plate, garnished with avocado and lemon slices. Serve immediately. Yield: 12 servings.

Right: Serve Frosty Tomato Salad balls, shaped with an ice cream scoop, straight from the freezer. Just add avocado slices and lettuce for Christmas color.

GRUYÈRE PUFFS

1 cup water
½ cup butter or margarine
1 cup all-purpose flour
⅛ teaspoon salt
4 eggs
1 cup (4 ounces) shredded Gruyère or
    Swiss cheese
1 teaspoon dried dillweed
¼ teaspoon ground nutmeg
1 egg
1 tablespoon water
Cubed ham (½-inch cubes)
Spanish pimiento-stuffed olives
Small pitted ripe olives

Combine 1 cup water and butter in a

heavy 2-quart saucepan; bring to a boil, stirring until butter melts. Add flour and salt, stirring vigorously until mixture leaves sides of pan and forms a smooth ball. Remove from heat, and cool 2 minutes. Add 4 eggs, one at a time, stirring vigorously with a wooden spoon after each addition until mixture is well blended. Beat in cheese, dillweed, and nutmeg.

Drop batter by heaping teaspoonfuls 3 inches apart onto greased baking sheets. Combine remaining egg and 1 tablespoon water, blending well. Brush top of each puff gently with egg mixture.

Bake at 400° for 15 minutes or until they are puffed and golden brown. Gently transfer the puffs to wire racks, and allow them to cool completely.

When cool, make an incision on side of each puff, using a sharp knife. Fill with choice of assorted centers. Place puffs in heavy-duty zip-top plastic bags or in freezer containers; seal, label, and freeze up to 1 month.

To serve, bake desired number of frozen puffs at 325° for 10 minutes or until hot. Yield: about 4 dozen.

PASTA MARINARA
½ pound hot Italian sausage, casings
    removed
1 medium onion, chopped
1 medium-size green pepper, chopped
2 cloves garlic, minced
2 tablespoons olive or vegetable oil
2 (14½-ounce) cans tomato wedges,
    undrained
1 (6-ounce) can tomato paste
2 boneless chicken breast halves, cooked
    and chopped
1 teaspoon dried basil leaves
1 teaspoon dried oregano leaves
½ teaspoon salt
½ (16-ounce) package bowtie pasta,
    cooked and drained
Grated Parmesan cheese (optional)

Brown sausage in a medium skillet, stirring

to crumble; drain and set aside. Sauté onion, green pepper, and garlic in oil in a small Dutch oven until tender. Add reserved sausage and next 6 ingredients; bring to a boil. Reduce heat, and simmer, stirring occasionally, 30 minutes.

Place pasta in a 13- x 9- x 2-inch baking dish; spoon sauce over pasta. Wrap securely with heavy-duty aluminum foil or freezer wrap. Freeze up to 6 weeks.

To serve, thaw overnight in refrigerator. Bake at 350° for 1 hour or until thoroughly heated. Let pasta stand 5 minutes before serving; sprinkle with Parmesan cheese if desired. Yield: 6 servings.

SAVORY BREW BRAID
2 packages dry yeast
1 tablespoon sugar
1½ cups warm water (105° to 115°)
1 cup warm beer (105° to 115°)
⅓ cup vegetable oil
2 teaspoons salt
6½ to 7 cups unbleached flour, divided
Savory Sausage Filling (recipe follows)

Dissolve yeast and sugar in water in a large bowl; let stand 5 minutes or until mixture is bubbly.

Add next 3 ingredients, stirring until well blended. Add 3 cups flour; stir well with a wooden spoon. Stir in enough of remaining flour to form a soft dough.

Turn dough out onto a lightly floured surface; knead 8 minutes or until smooth and elastic. Place dough in a greased bowl, turning to grease top. Cover and let rise in a warm place (85°), free from drafts, for 45

Right: Spicy sausage filling is not the only surprise in this golden-crusted Savory Brew Braid. Easy to prepare in advance, this bread will keep up to six weeks in the freezer. For stunning results, simply cut dough in strips and fold over, as shown in inset.

minutes or until doubled in bulk. Punch dough down; cover and let rest 10 minutes.

Divide dough into 3 equal portions. Working with 1 portion at a time, roll dough to a 12- x 8-inch rectangle on a lightly floured surface. Spread one-third of Savory Sausage Filling down entire center length of dough. Cut dough along sides of filling into ½-inch strips. Fold strips, one at a time, at an angle over filling, alternating from side to side in a braid-like fashion. Gently transfer loaf to a lightly greased baking sheet; repeat procedure with remaining 2 portions of dough and Savory Sausage Filling. Let rise, uncovered, in a warm place (85°), free from drafts, 45 minutes. (Loaves will not double in bulk.) Bake at 400° for 25 minutes or until golden brown. Gently transfer loaves to wire racks, and cool completely. Wrap securely in heavy-duty aluminum foil or freezer wrap; label and freeze up to 6 weeks.

To serve, thaw loaves overnight in refrigerator. Bake at 325° for 1 hour or until thoroughly heated. Do not overheat. Slice and serve immediately. Yield: 3 loaves.

Savory Sausage Filling:
1 pound hot or mild Italian sausage, casings removed
1 cup sunflower kernels
2 tablespoons olive oil
¼ cup chopped onion
2 cloves garlic, minced
1 (10-ounce) package frozen chopped spinach, thawed, drained, and squeezed dry
1 cup ricotta cheese
2 teaspoons dried basil leaves
¼ teaspoon freshly ground pepper

Crumble sausage in a large skillet. Cook over medium heat until meat is browned. Drain and pat dry between paper towels; set aside.

Cook sunflower kernels in oil in a large skillet over medium heat until golden. Stir in onion and garlic; sauté until tender.

Combine cooked sausage, sunflower kernel mixture, and remaining ingredients in a large

bowl, stirring until well blended. Yield: about 1 quart.

FESTIVE RASPBERRY SALAD
1 (10-ounce) package frozen raspberries, thawed
1 cup whipping cream
½ cup sifted powdered sugar
Dash of salt
1 (8-ounce) can crushed pineapple, drained
½ cup chopped walnuts
½ cup chopped celery
Lettuce leaves

Press raspberries through food mill or a fine mesh sieve. Discard seeds; set raspberry puree aside.

Beat whipping cream until foamy; add sugar and salt. Beat until soft peaks form. Fold in reserved raspberry puree. Freeze 1 hour or until icy and almost firm. Beat at medium speed of electric mixer until fluffy. Stir in pineapple, walnuts, and celery. Spoon mixture into 8 lightly oiled ½-cup ring molds or a 4-cup mold; freeze up to 1 month.

To serve, unmold frozen salads onto lettuce-lined serving plates. Let stand 5 minutes before serving. Yield: 8 servings.

CRANBERRY COCONUT CHUTNEY
4 cups fresh cranberries
¾ cup firmly packed brown sugar
½ cup orange juice
2 tablespoons minced dried onion
2 tablespoons vinegar
½ teaspoon ground cinnamon
¼ teaspoon ground ginger
2 medium pears or apples, cored, unpeeled, and chopped
½ cup flaked coconut

Combine first 7 ingredients in a medium Dutch oven; stir well. Cook, uncovered, over medium heat 6 to 8 minutes or until cranberries pop. Add pears; cook 5 minutes or until tender. Stir in coconut.

Cool chutney to room temperature; spoon into a heavy-duty zip-top plastic bag or freezer container. Seal, label, and freeze up to one month.

To serve, thaw chutney overnight in refrigerator, and serve chilled with roasted ham or turkey. Yield: 1 quart.

Microwave Conversion:

Combine first 7 ingredients in a 2-quart glass bowl; stir well. Cover and microwave at HIGH for 4 to 6 minutes, or until cranberries begin to pop, stirring twice. Add pears; microwave at HIGH 2 minutes or until tender. Stir in coconut.

Cool chutney to room temperature; freeze and serve as directed above.

SMOKED CHEDDAR AND ONION TART
¼ cup chopped carrot
¼ cup chopped celery
1 large yellow onion, coarsely chopped
1 tablespoon butter or margarine
3 eggs, beaten
1 cup half-and-half
1½ cups (6 ounces) smoked Cheddar
   cheese
½ cup minced prosciutto or ham
⅛ teaspoon salt
Pinch of ground nutmeg
Smoked Cheddar Pastry (recipe follows)
Carrot curls
Fresh parsley sprigs

Sauté carrot, celery, and onion in butter in a small skillet until tender. Combine sautéed vegetables, eggs, half-and-half, cheese, ham, salt, and nutmeg in a large bowl; stir until well blended, and set aside.

Roll chilled Smoked Cheddar Pastry to ⅛-inch thickness on a lightly floured surface. Fit pastry into a 9-inch tart pan; trim excess pastry around edges. Fold edges under, and flute as desired.

Spoon cheese mixture into prepared pastry shell. Wrap tart securely in heavy-duty aluminum foil or freezer wrap; label and freeze up to 1 month.

To serve, thaw tart overnight in refrigerator. Bake at 325° for 1 hour or until set. Cool on a wire rack. Serve warm or at room temperature; garnish with carrot curls and parsley sprigs. Yield: one 9-inch tart.

Smoked Cheddar Pastry:
1¼ cups all-purpose flour
¼ teaspoon salt
Dash of red pepper
⅓ cup plus 2 tablespoons shortening
½ cup (2 ounces) finely shredded smoked
   Cheddar cheese
3 to 4 tablespoons cold water

Combine flour, salt, and red pepper in a medium bowl; cut in shortening and cheese, using a pastry blender, until mixture resembles coarse meal. Sprinkle water evenly over surface. Stir with a fork until dry ingredients are moistened. Shape dough into a ball; chill. Yield: enough pastry for one 9-inch tart.

MEXICAN CHILI
1½ pounds ground beef chuck
½ pound bulk pork sausage
1 medium onion, chopped
1 green pepper, chopped
2 cloves garlic, minced
1 (14½-ounce) can stewed tomatoes,
   undrained
1 (6-ounce) can tomato paste
1 cup beef broth or water
3 tablespoons chili powder
1 teaspoon ground cumin
½ teaspoon salt
½ teaspoon freshly ground pepper
1 (15-ounce) can kidney beans, drained
1 (1-ounce) square unsweetened
   chocolate, chopped
Warm buttered flour tortillas

Combine ground chuck, sausage, onion, green pepper, and garlic in a large Dutch oven; cook over medium heat until meat is browned, stirring to crumble. Drain well and stir in next 7 ingredients. Cover and simmer

1 hour, stirring occasionally. Add beans and chocolate; simmer 20 additional minutes.

Cool chili to room temperature, and spoon into a large heavy-duty zip-top plastic bag or freezer container. Seal, label, and freeze up to 6 weeks. To serve, heat desired amount. Serve with flour tortillas. Yield: 8 cups.

Microwave Conversion:

Crumble ground chuck and sausage in a 3-quart casserole, and add next 3 ingredients. Cover with casserole lid or heavy-duty plastic wrap. Microwave at HIGH 6 to 8 minutes or until meat is browned, stirring every 2 minutes. Drain well.

Stir in remaining ingredients except beans and chocolate. Cover and microwave at HIGH for 10 minutes; add chocolate and beans, stirring well. Cover and microwave at MEDIUM (50% power) for 25 to 30 minutes, stirring every 10 minutes.

Cool chili to room temperature; spoon chili into a large heavy-duty zip-top plastic bag or freezer container. Seal, label, and freeze. Serve as directed above.

MUSHROOM SPINACH SOUFFLÉS
1 pound fresh spinach, washed and
   trimmed
½ pound fresh mushrooms, coarsely
   chopped
¼ cup plus 2 tablespoons butter or
   margarine
¼ cup plus 2 tablespoons all-purpose
   flour
2 cups whipping cream
½ cup grated Parmesan cheese
½ teaspoon salt
½ teaspoon freshly ground pepper
Olive oil
6 eggs, separated

Place spinach in a steamer basket or metal colander. Place over boiling water; cover and steam 10 minutes. Drain well, and pat dry between paper towels. Finely chop spinach, and set aside.

Sauté the mushrooms in butter in a large skillet until tender. Transfer mushrooms to a small bowl, using a slotted spoon; set aside. Add flour to melted butter, stirring until smooth. Cook 1 minute, stirring constantly. Gradually add cream, stirring constantly over medium heat until thickened and bubbly. Remove from heat, and stir in reserved spinach, mushrooms, cheese, salt, and pepper. Set aside.

Lightly grease six 10-ounce custard cups with olive oil, and set aside. Beat egg whites (at room temperature) until stiff peaks form. Beat egg yolks in a large mixing bowl until thick and pale (about 5 minutes); stir in reserved spinach mixture. Gradually fold beaten egg whites into spinach mixture. Spoon evenly into prepared custard cups. Cover each with heavy-duty aluminum foil or freezer wrap; label and freeze up to 1 month.

To serve, thaw soufflés overnight in refrigerator. Remove foil, and bake at 350° for 45 minutes or until puffed and brown. Serve immediately. Yield: 6 servings.

Note: Soufflés may be baked frozen at 350° for 1 hour or until puffed and brown.

HOLIDAY PUMPKIN SOUP
½ cup chopped onion
¼ cup chopped celery
1 clove garlic, minced
3 tablespoons butter or margarine
4 cups chicken broth
1 (16-ounce) can cooked, mashed
   pumpkin
1 cup milk
¼ cup all-purpose flour
⅓ cup sherry
½ teaspoon salt
Chopped fresh chives

Sauté onion, celery, and garlic in butter in a medium Dutch oven until tender. Add chicken broth and pumpkin, stirring until smooth. Bring to a boil; reduce heat, and simmer 15 minutes, stirring occasionally.

Combine milk and flour in a small mixing bowl; stir with a wire whisk until well

blended. Stir flour mixture into soup; cook until slightly thickened, stirring occasionally. Remove from heat; stir in sherry and salt.

Cool soup to room temperature; pour into heavy-duty zip-top plastic bags or freezer containers. Seal, label, and freeze up to six weeks.

To serve, thaw soup and heat. Garnish with chopped fresh chives. Yield: about 1½ quarts.

Microwave Conversion:

Combine first 4 ingredients in a large glass bowl. Cover with heavy-duty plastic wrap, and microwave at HIGH for 2 minutes. Add chicken broth and pumpkin, stirring until well blended; cover with heavy-duty plastic

Above: Creamy, golden Holiday Pumpkin Soup, served with bread, can be a complete meal which takes only minutes to serve.

wrap, and microwave at HIGH for 2 minutes or until mixture is warm.

Combine milk and flour in a small bowl; stir until well blended. Stir flour mixture into soup, and cover with heavy-duty plastic wrap. Microwave at HIGH for 28 to 30 minutes, stirring every 6 minutes. Stir in sherry and salt. Freeze as directed above.

To serve, thaw and reheat pumpkin soup in a microwave at MEDIUM (50% power), stirring occasionally.

125

PATTERNS

A MERRY MITTEN QUILT
Instructions are on page 20.
Patterns are full-size.

TRIM A TABLETOP DOWEL TREE
Instructions are on page 30.
Patterns are full-size.

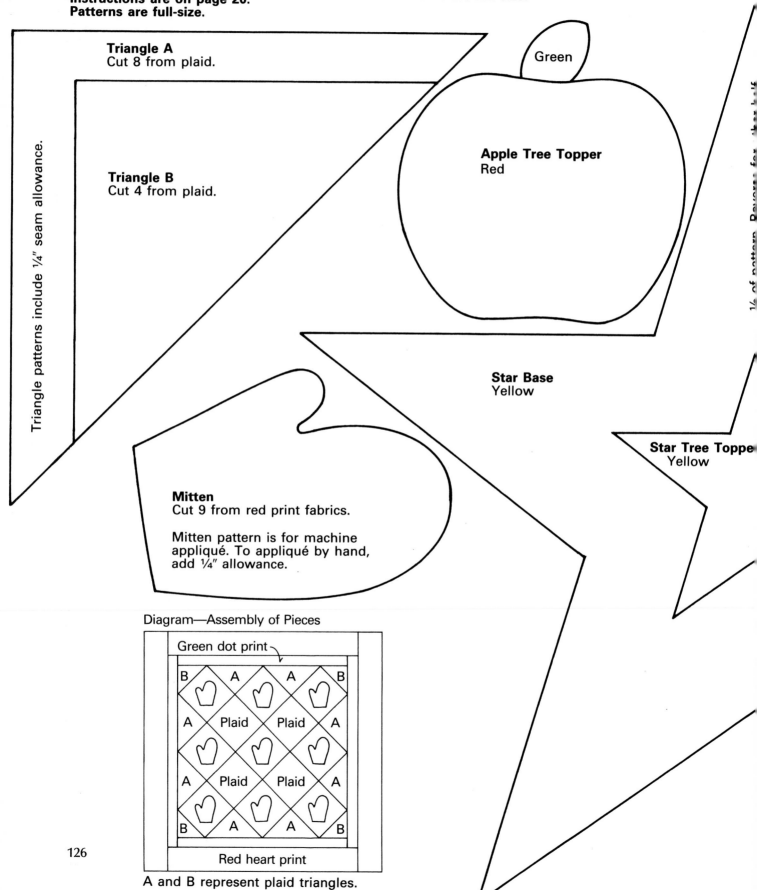

Triangle patterns include ¼" seam allowance.

Triangle A
Cut 8 from plaid.

Triangle B
Cut 4 from plaid.

Mitten
Cut 9 from red print fabrics.

Mitten pattern is for machine appliqué. To appliqué by hand, add ¼" allowance.

Green

Apple Tree Topper
Red

Star Base
Yellow

Star Tree Topper
Yellow

Diagram—Assembly of Pieces

Green dot print

B	A		A	B
A	Plaid		Plaid	A
A	Plaid		Plaid	A
B	A		A	B

Red heart print

A and B represent plaid triangles.

126

THREE JOLLY SNOWMEN
Instructions are on page 22.
Patterns are full-size.

Diagram—Snowman Layout

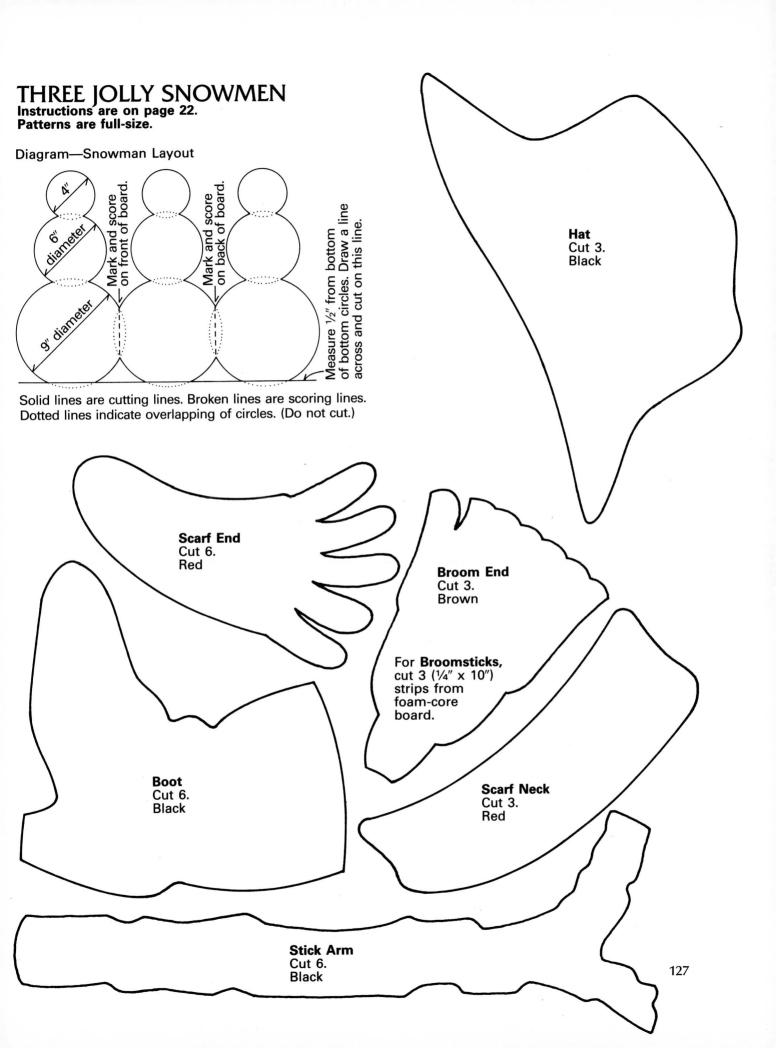

4"

6" diameter

9" diameter

Mark and score on front of board.

Mark and score on back of board.

Measure ½" from bottom of bottom circles. Draw a line across and cut on this line.

Solid lines are cutting lines. Broken lines are scoring lines.
Dotted lines indicate overlapping of circles. (Do not cut.)

Hat
Cut 3.
Black

Scarf End
Cut 6.
Red

Broom End
Cut 3.
Brown

For **Broomsticks**, cut 3 (¼" x 10") strips from foam-core board.

Boot
Cut 6.
Black

Scarf Neck
Cut 3.
Red

Stick Arm
Cut 6.
Black

127

A VICTORIAN TREE
Instructions begin on page 24.
Patterns are full-size.

SWAN TREE SKIRT
Instructions are on page 24.
Patterns are full-size.

Swan
Cut 7.

Match dots and
continue pattern.

X
Bow

Wing Placement

Match dots and continue pattern.

Glue garland between Xs.

128

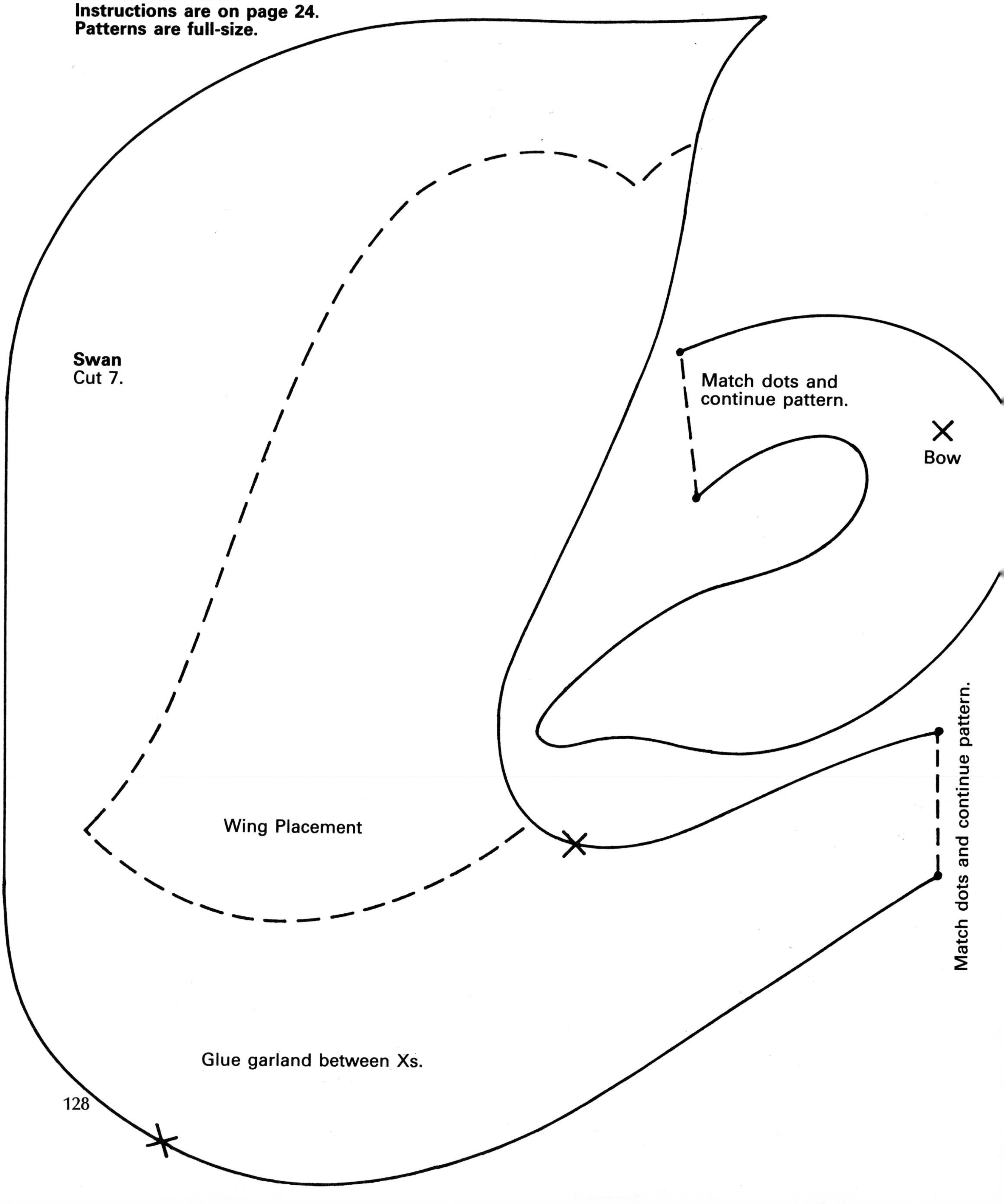

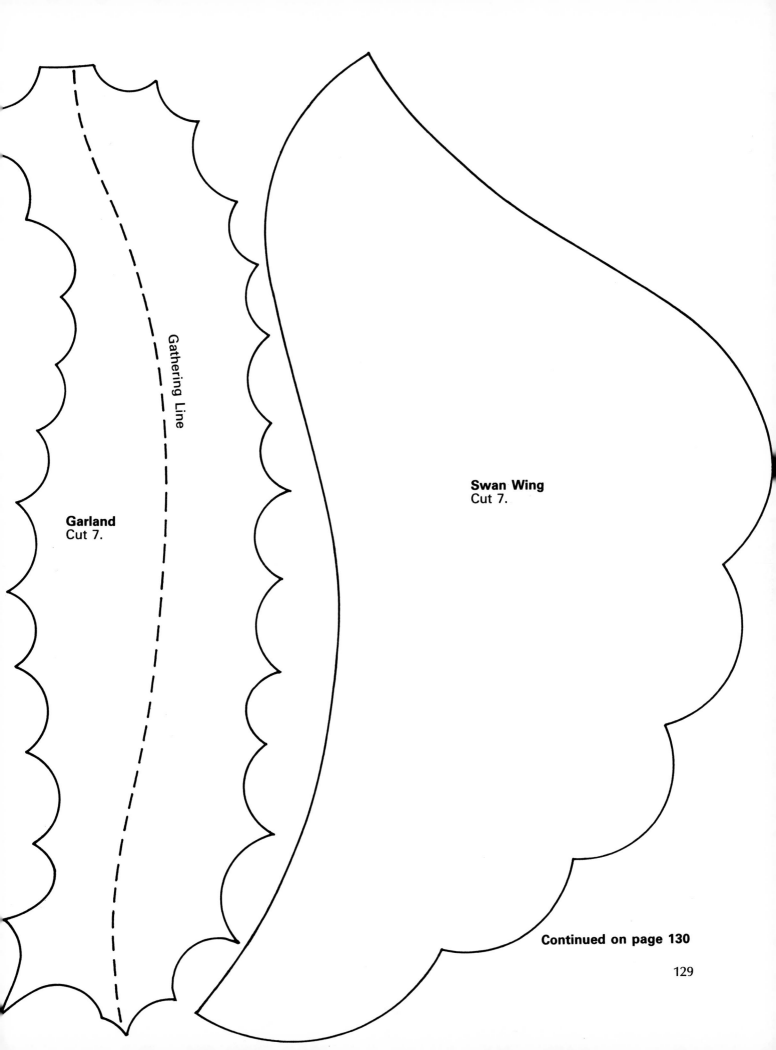

Garland
Cut 7.

Gathering Line

Swan Wing
Cut 7.

Continued on page 130

129

A VICTORIAN TREE (Continued)

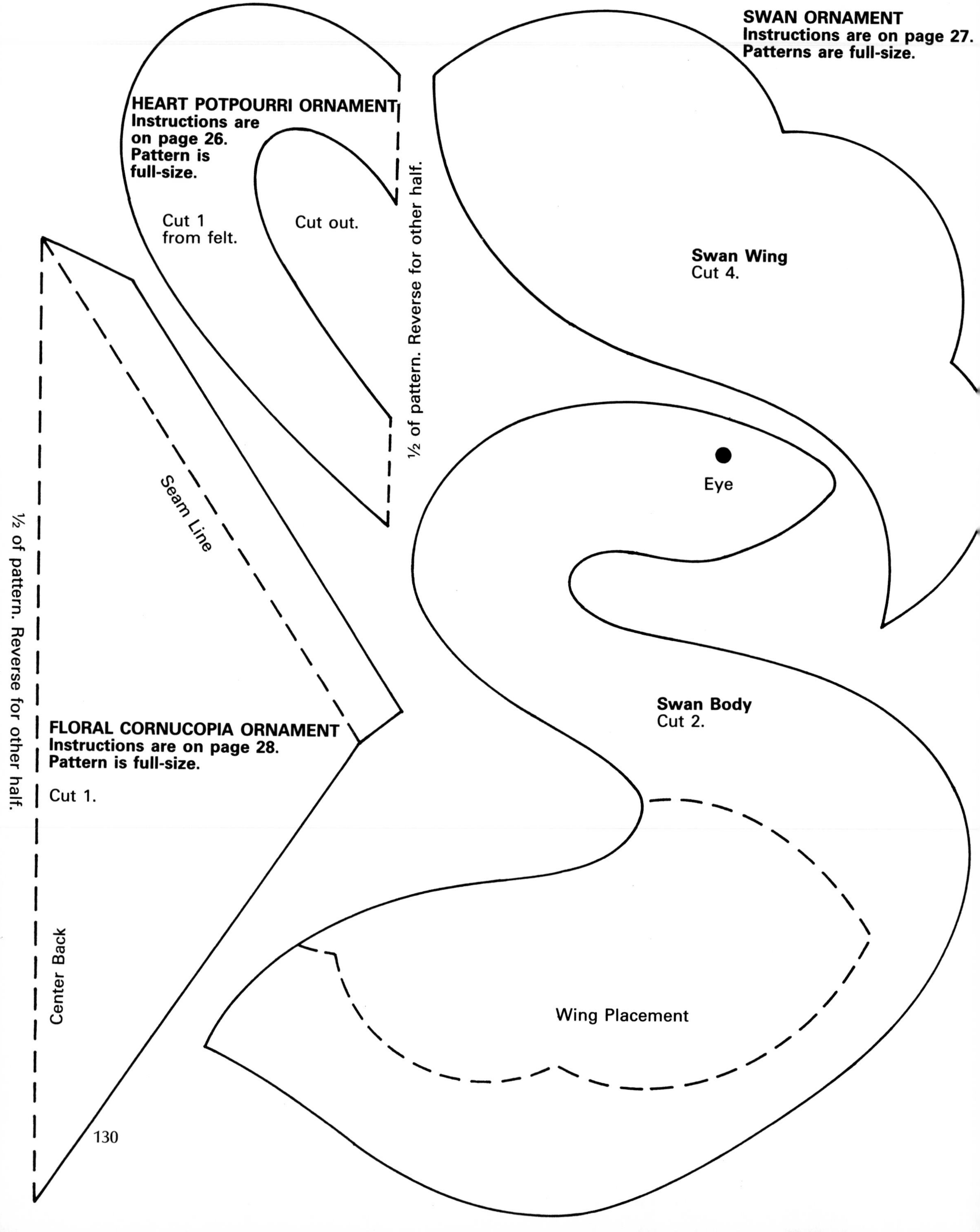

HEART POTPOURRI ORNAMENT
Instructions are
on page 26.
Pattern is
full-size.

Cut 1
from felt.

Cut out.

½ of pattern. Reverse for other half.

SWAN ORNAMENT
Instructions are on page 27.
Patterns are full-size.

Swan Wing
Cut 4.

Eye

Seam Line

½ of pattern. Reverse for other half.

Swan Body
Cut 2.

FLORAL CORNUCOPIA ORNAMENT
Instructions are on page 28.
Pattern is full-size.

Cut 1.

Center Back

Wing Placement

130

HOUSE-IN-THE-SNOW STOCKING

Instructions are on page 32.
Patterns are full-size.
Add ¼″ seam allowance
to all pattern pieces.

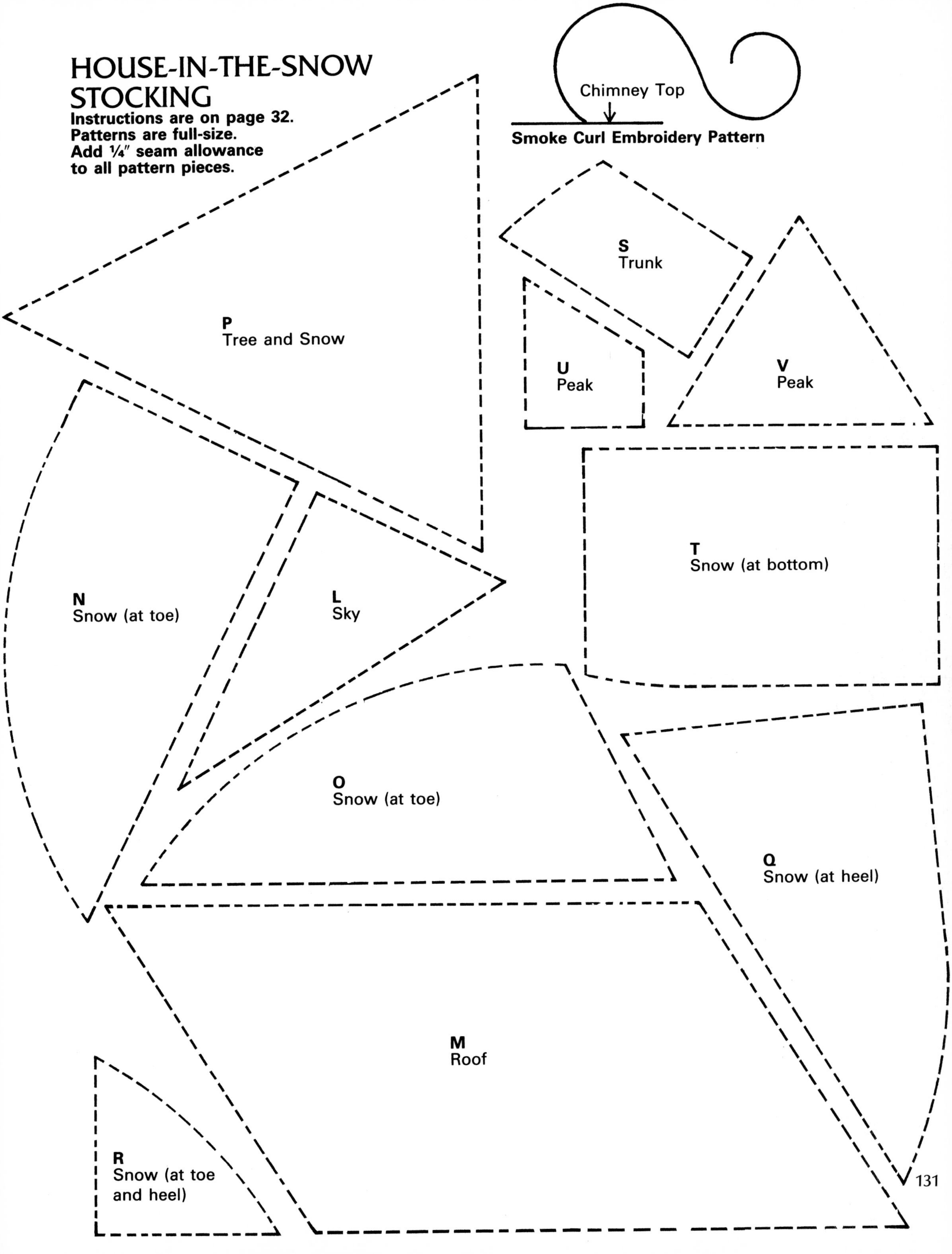

Chimney Top

Smoke Curl Embroidery Pattern

P
Tree and Snow

S
Trunk

U
Peak

V
Peak

T
Snow (at bottom)

N
Snow (at toe)

L
Sky

O
Snow (at toe)

Q
Snow (at heel)

M
Roof

R
Snow (at toe
and heel)

131

SPRIGHTLY SANTA COUPLE
Instructions are on page 35.
Patterns are full-size.
Add 1" seam allowance around patterns.

Mr. Santa
Cut 2.

Stitch at Xs and
pull stitches
tight for added
definition.

132

Mrs. Santa
Cut 2.

Stitch at Xs and
pull stitches
tight for added
definition.

133

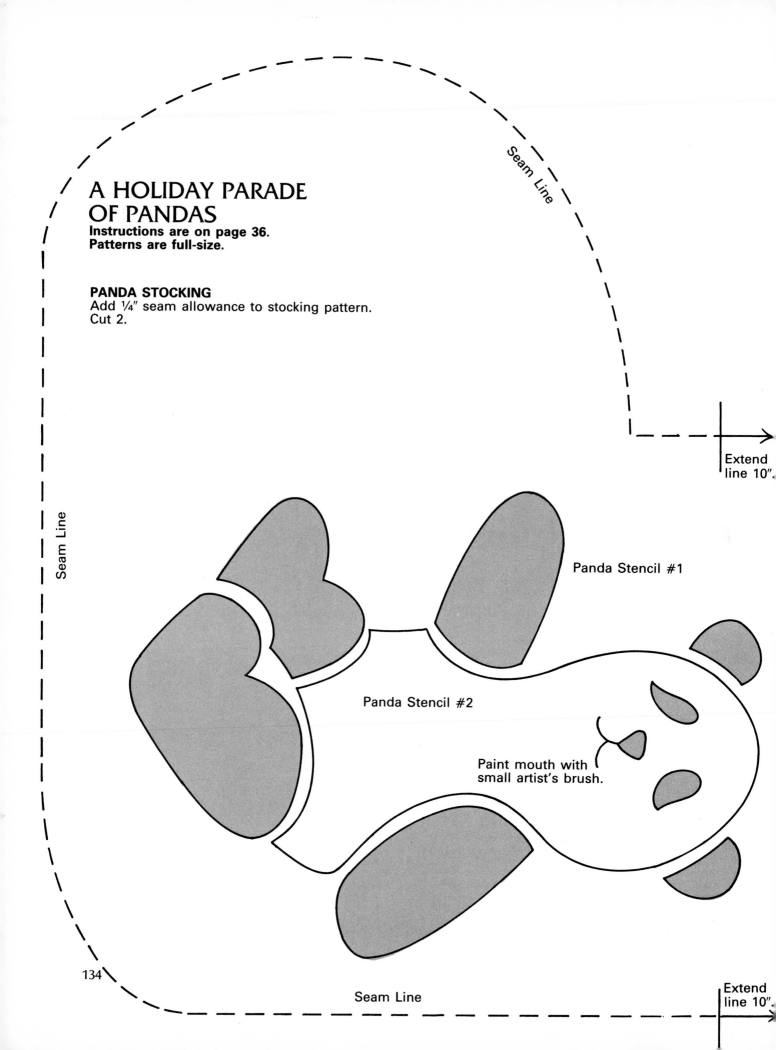

Seam Line

A HOLIDAY PARADE OF PANDAS
**Instructions are on page 36.
Patterns are full-size.**

PANDA STOCKING
Add ¼″ seam allowance to stocking pattern.
Cut 2.

Seam Line

Extend
line 10″.

Panda Stencil #1

Panda Stencil #2

Paint mouth with
small artist's brush.

Seam Line

Extend
line 10″.

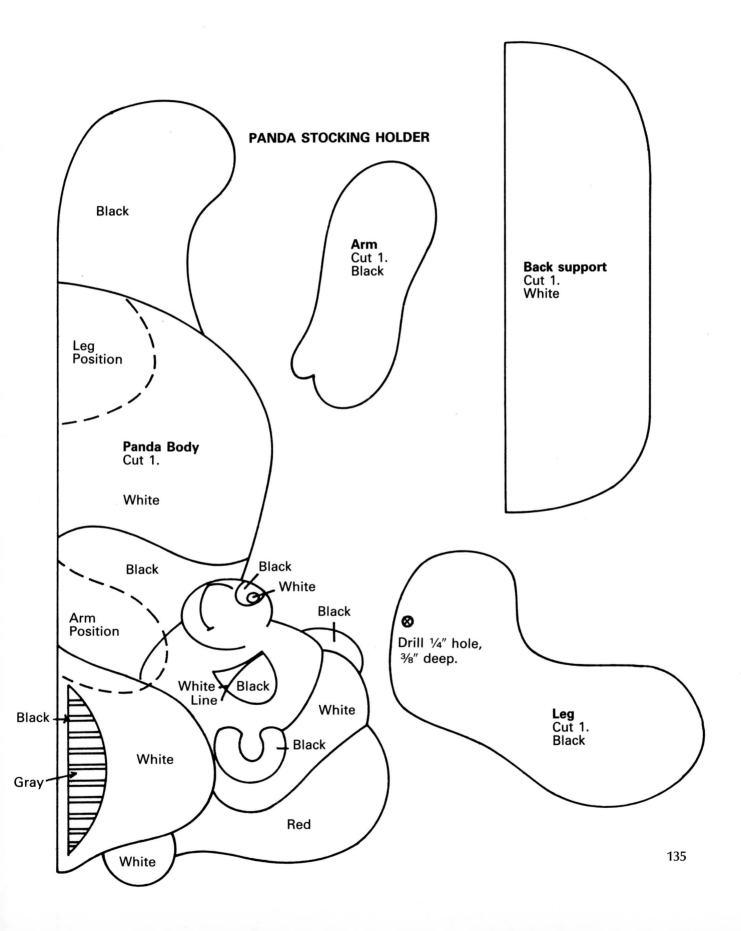

PANDA STOCKING HOLDER

Black

Arm
Cut 1.
Black

Back support
Cut 1.
White

Leg
Position

Panda Body
Cut 1.

White

Black

Black

White

Black

Arm
Position

White
Line

Black

Drill ¼" hole,
⅜" deep.

Black

Gray

White

White

Black

Leg
Cut 1.
Black

Red

White

135

PAPER SERAPH
Instructions are on page 40.
Patterns are full-size.

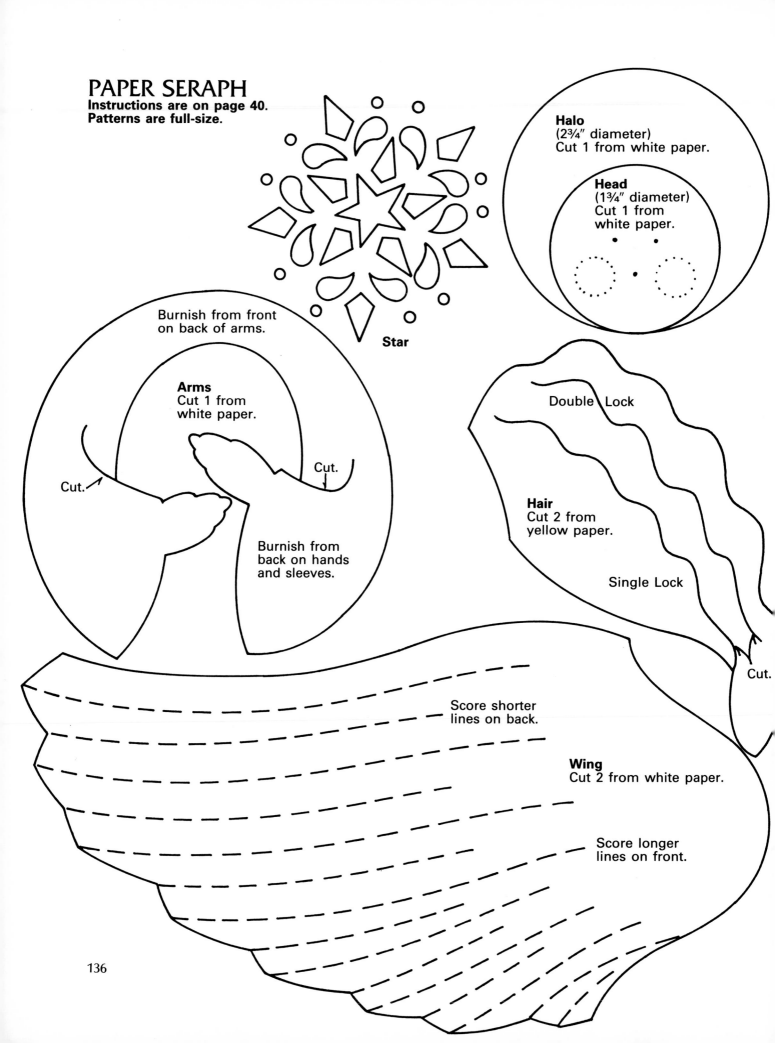

Star

Halo
(2¾″ diameter)
Cut 1 from white paper.

Head
(1¾″ diameter)
Cut 1 from
white paper.

Burnish from front
on back of arms.

Arms
Cut 1 from
white paper.

Cut.

Cut.

Burnish from
back on hands
and sleeves.

Double Lock

Hair
Cut 2 from
yellow paper.

Single Lock

Cut.

Score shorter
lines on back.

Wing
Cut 2 from white paper.

Score longer
lines on front.

136

A CHRISTMAS CHERUB
Instructions are on page 42.
Patterns are full-size.
Patterns include ⅛″ seam allowance.

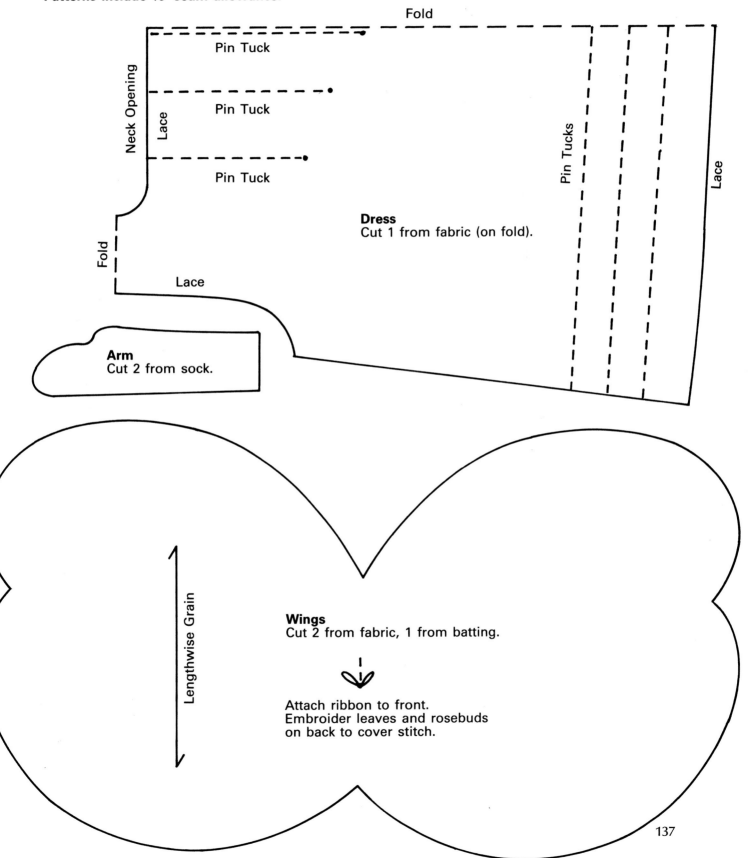

Fold

Pin Tuck

Neck Opening

Lace

Pin Tuck

Pin Tuck

Pin Tucks

Lace

Fold

Lace

Dress
Cut 1 from fabric (on fold).

Arm
Cut 2 from sock.

Lengthwise Grain

Wings
Cut 2 from fabric, 1 from batting.

Attach ribbon to front.
Embroider leaves and rosebuds
on back to cover stitch.

137

CELESTIAL CHARM
CRAFTED FROM WOOD
Instructions are on page 45.
Patterns are full-size.

Note: **Clouds** and **Wings** are cut from the same pattern.

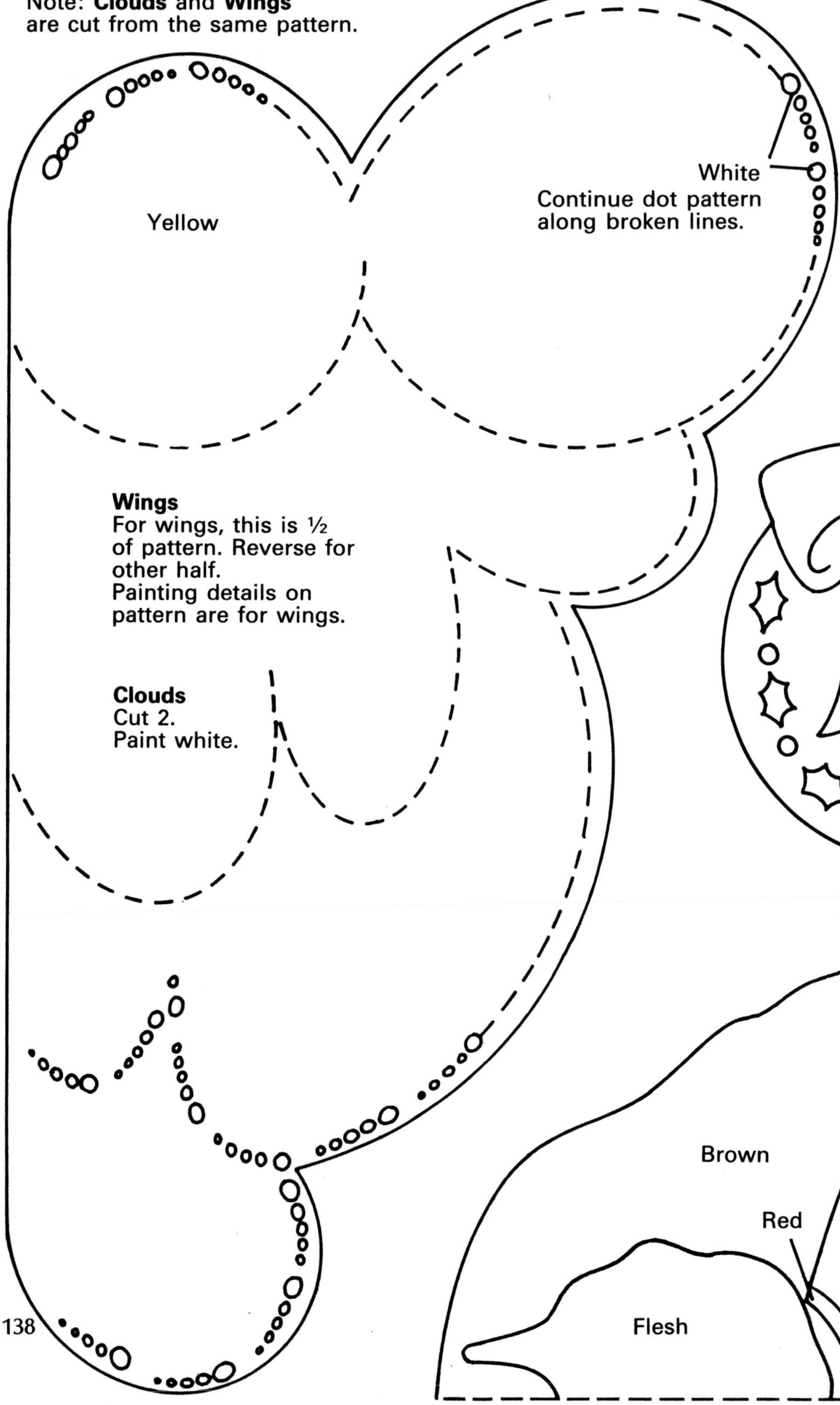

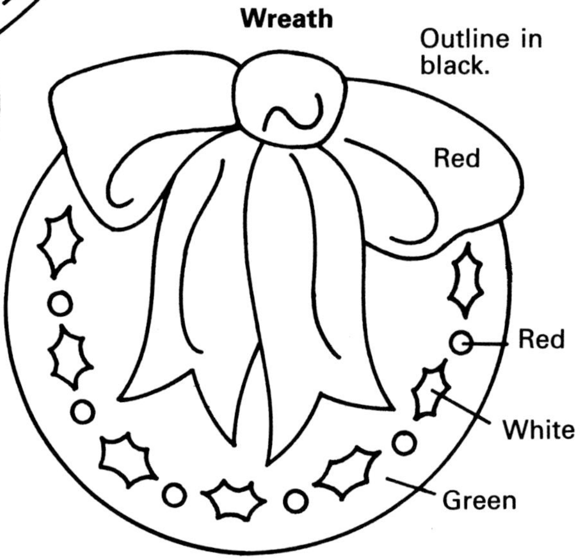

Yellow

White
Continue dot pattern along broken lines.

White

Halo
Yellow
Continue dot pattern along broken line.

Wings
For wings, this is ½ of pattern. Reverse for other half.
Painting details on pattern are for wings.

Clouds
Cut 2.
Paint white.

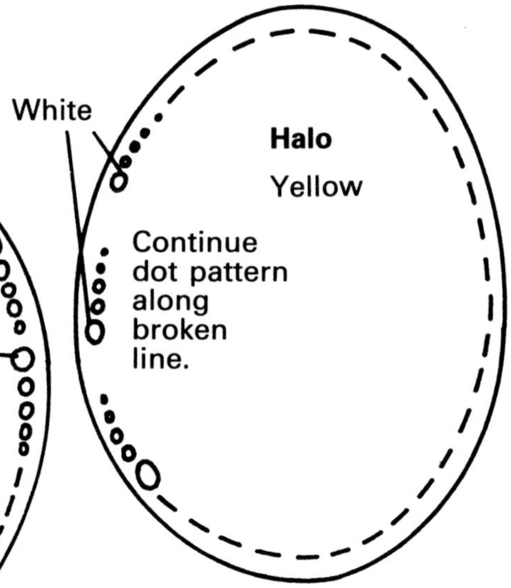

Wreath
Outline in black.

Red

Red

White

Green

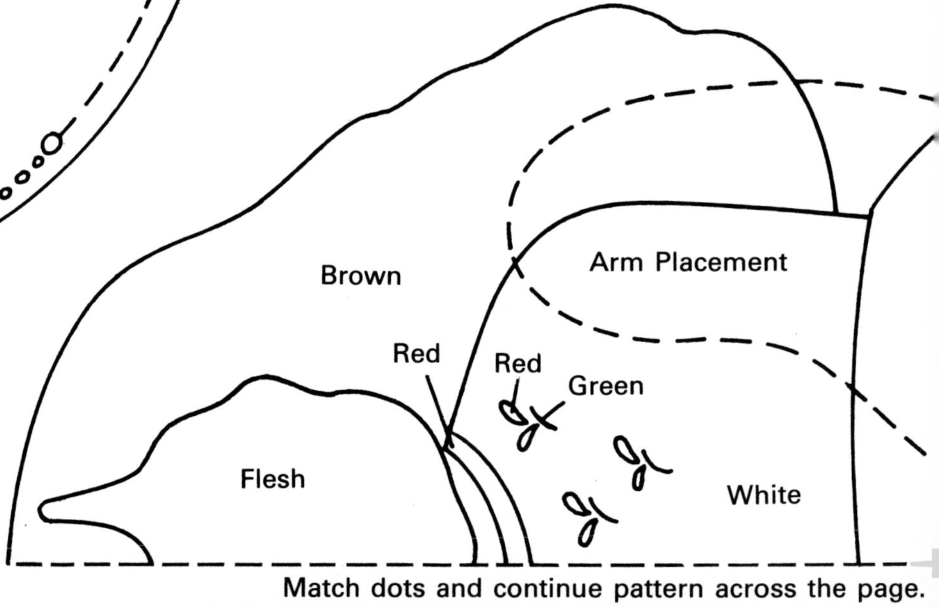

Brown

Arm Placement

Red

Red

Green

Flesh

White

138

Match dots and continue pattern across the page.

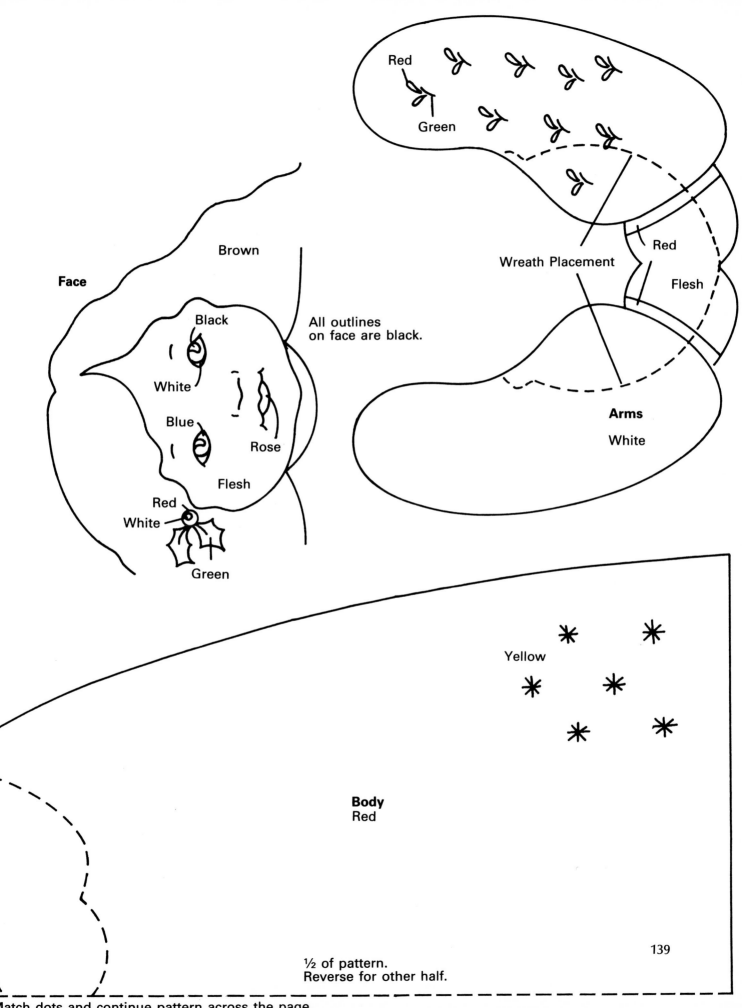

Red

Green

Face

Brown

Black

White

Blue

Rose

Flesh

Red

White

Green

All outlines
on face are black.

Wreath Placement

Red

Flesh

Arms

White

Yellow

Body
Red

139

½ of pattern.
Reverse for other half.

Match dots and continue pattern across the page.

ANGEL CRITTERS

Instructions are on page 46.
Patterns are full-size.
Patterns include ¼" seam allowance.

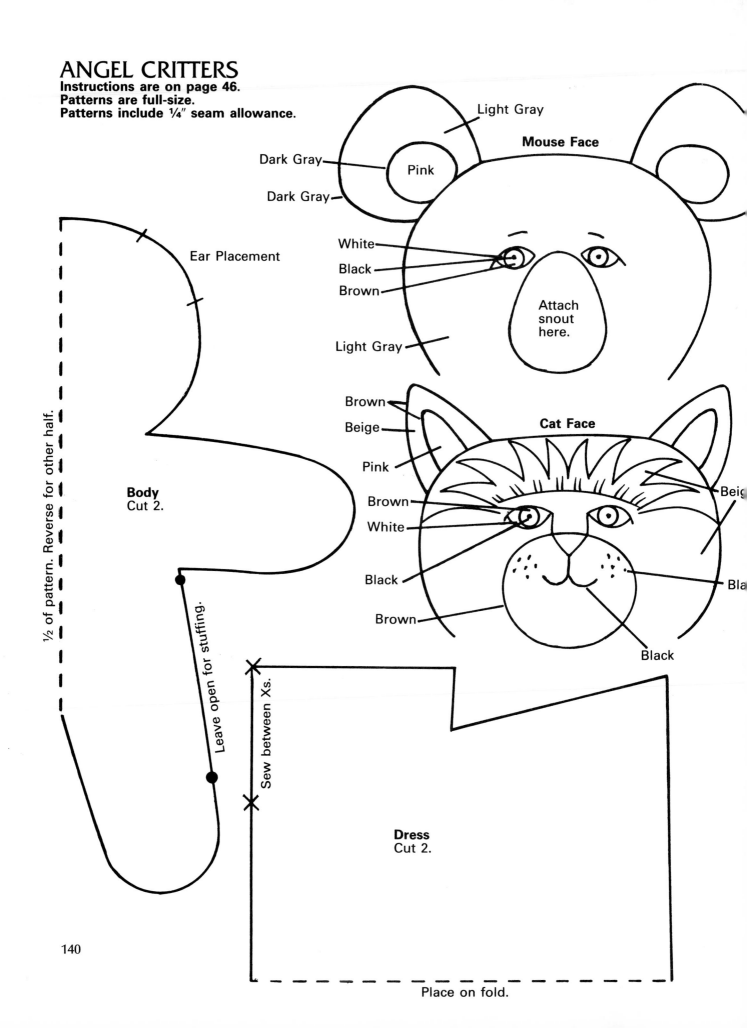

Light Gray

Mouse Face

Dark Gray

Pink

Dark Gray

White

Black

Brown

Ear Placement

Light Gray

Attach snout here.

½ of pattern. Reverse for other half.

Body
Cut 2.

Leave open for stuffing.

Brown

Beige

Pink

Brown

White

Black

Brown

Cat Face

Bei[g]

Bla[ck]

Black

Sew between Xs.

Dress
Cut 2.

Place on fold.

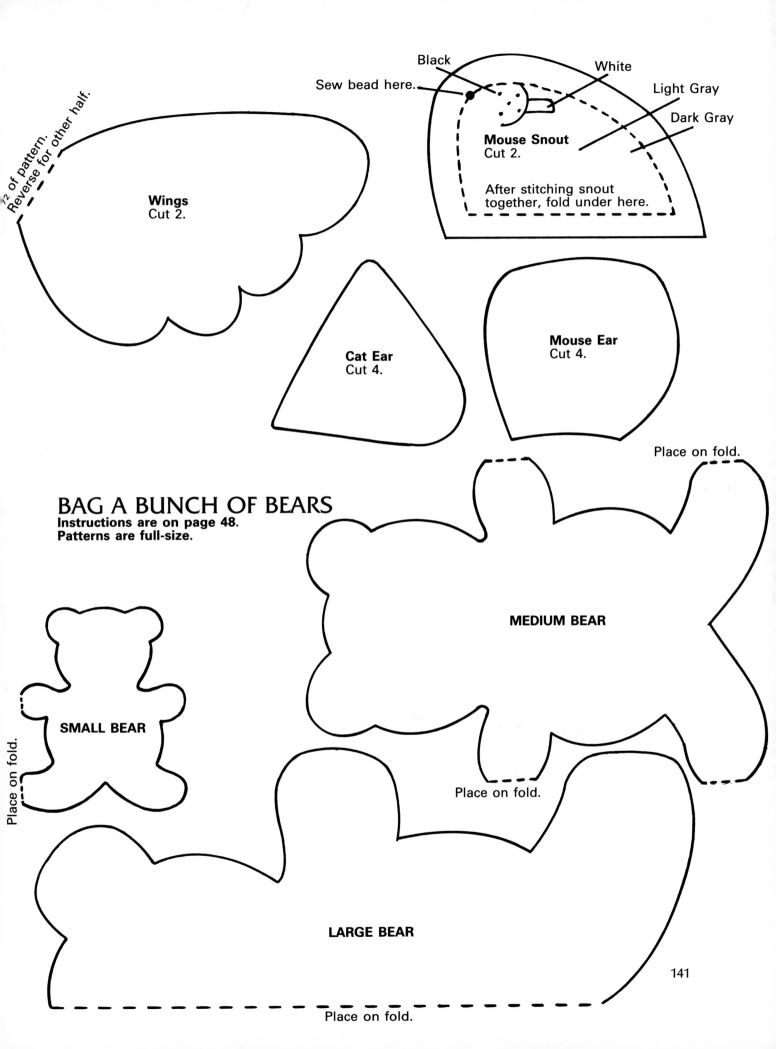

Black
Sew bead here.
White
Light Gray
Dark Gray

Mouse Snout
Cut 2.

After stitching snout together, fold under here.

½ of pattern. Reverse for other half.

Wings
Cut 2.

Cat Ear
Cut 4.

Mouse Ear
Cut 4.

Place on fold.

BAG A BUNCH OF BEARS
Instructions are on page 48.
Patterns are full-size.

MEDIUM BEAR

SMALL BEAR

Place on fold.

Place on fold.

LARGE BEAR

141

Place on fold.

REFLECTIONS OF THE SEASON

Instructions are on page 50.
Patterns are full-size.

ANGEL CARD

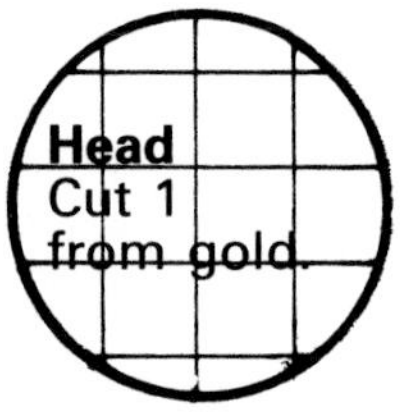

Head
Cut 1
from gold.

For eyes, cut a
green square in
half diagonally.

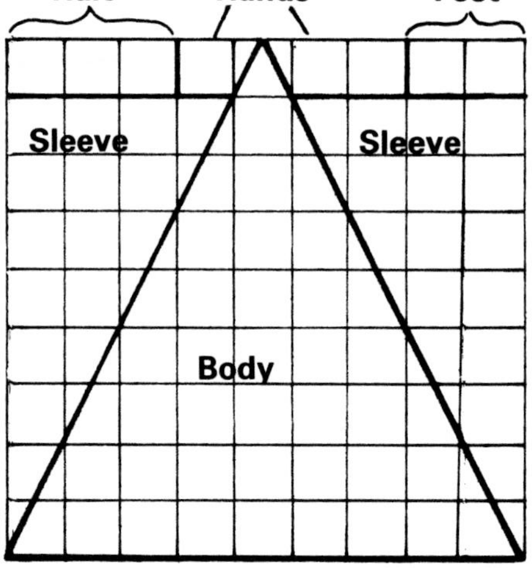

Halo   Hands   Feet

Sleeve   Sleeve

Body

Cut 1 from gold.

CHRISTMAS TREE CARD

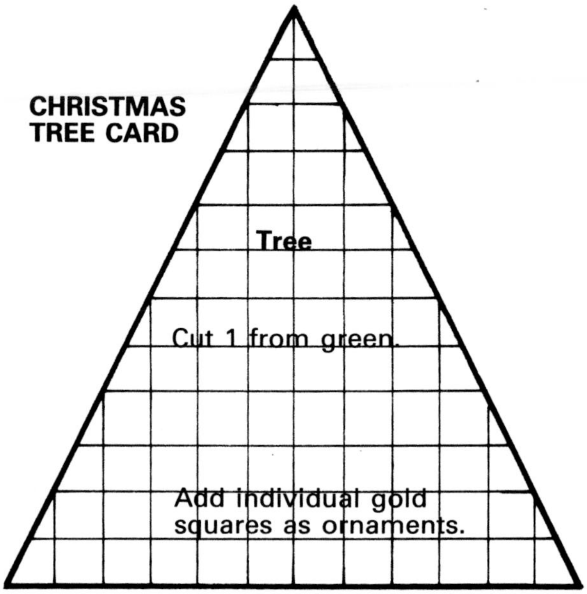

Tree

Cut 1 from green.

Add individual gold
squares as ornaments.

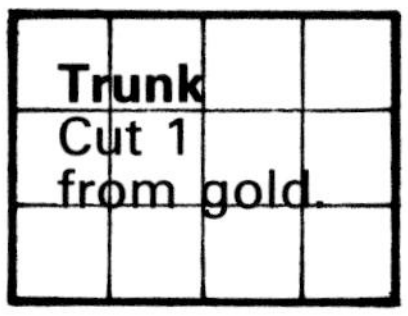

Trunk
Cut 1
from gold.

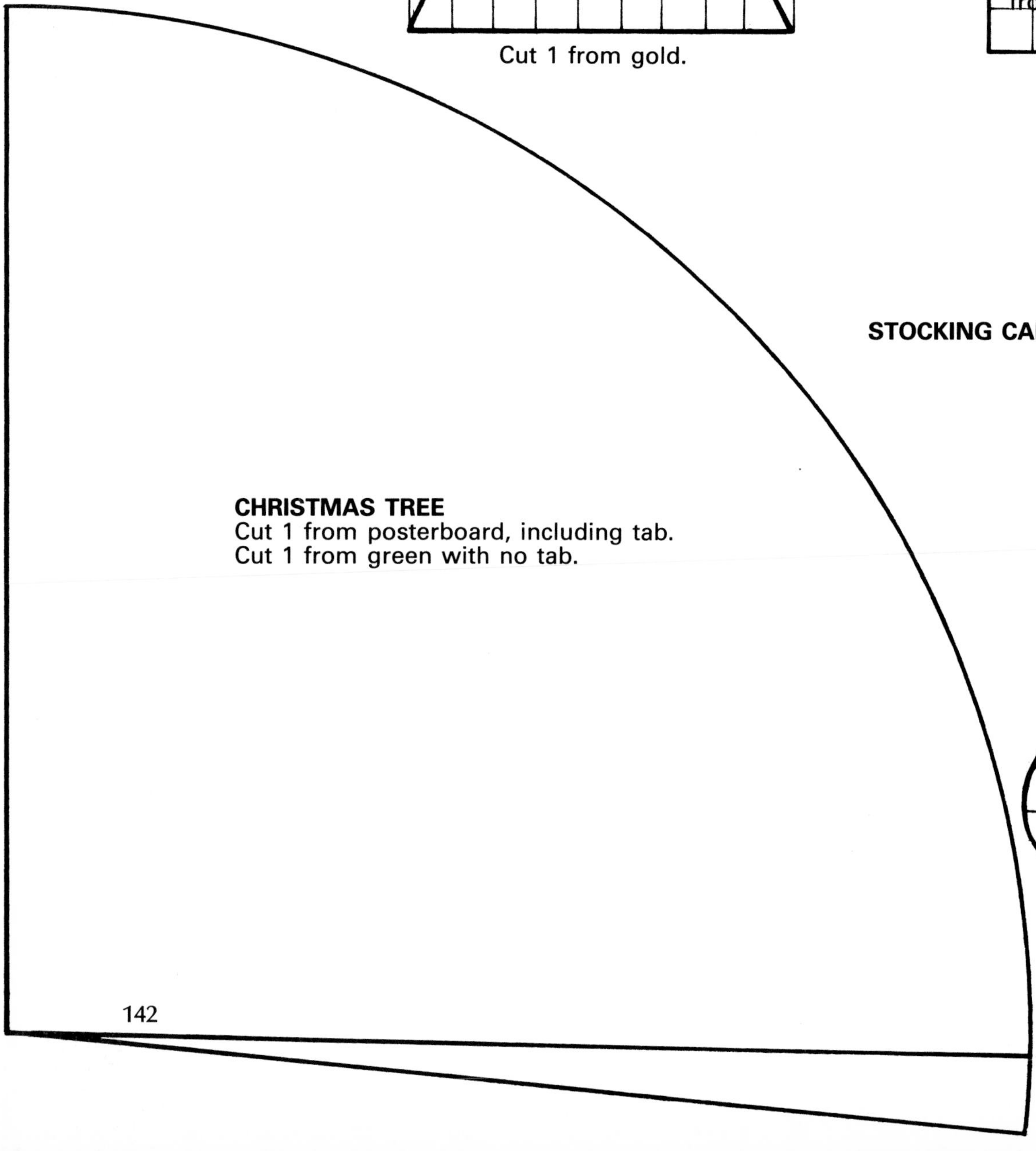

Stocking Cuff
Cut 1 from green.

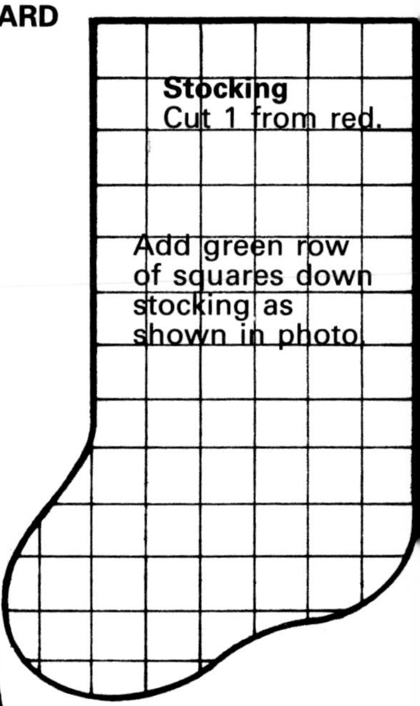

STOCKING CARD

Stocking
Cut 1 from red.

Add green row
of squares down
stocking as
shown in photo.

CHRISTMAS TREE
Cut 1 from posterboard, including tab.
Cut 1 from green with no tab.

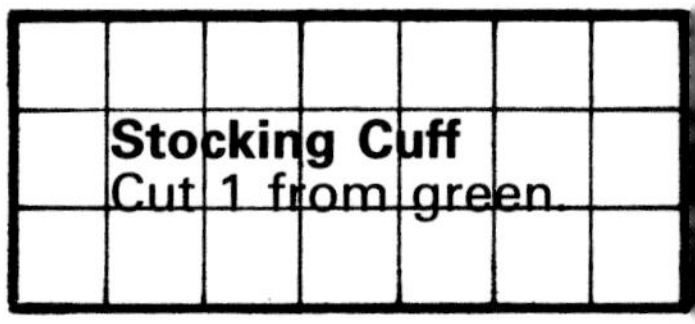

ORNAMENTS: MAKE ONE, MAKE ALL
Instructions begin on page 52.

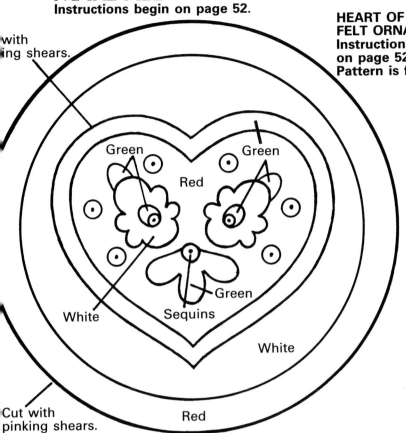

with
ing shears.

Green   Green

Red

Green

White   Sequins

White

Cut with
pinking shears.   Red

**HEART OF
FELT ORNAMENT**
Instructions are
on page 52.
Pattern is full-size.

HO HO HO ORNAMENT
Instructions are on page 55.
Chart for Plastic Canvas

⅓ of pattern. Repeat design 2 more
times, placing line AB on line CD.

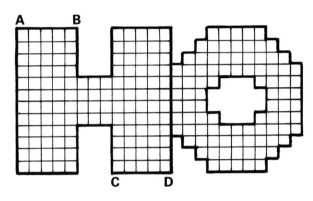

A   B

C   D

CHRISTMAS SEAL ORNAMENT
Instructions are on page 52.
Cross-Stitch Chart

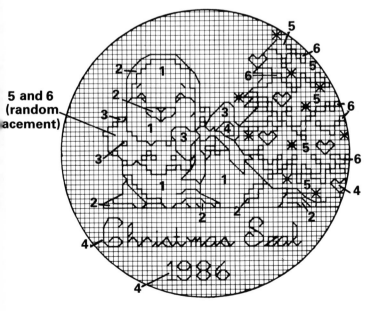

5 and 6
(random
placement)

Color Key
Note: If line on chart
crosses square on the
diagonal, stitch only half
the cross in that square.

1—White
2—Cream
3—Bright Red
4—Dark Red
5—Light Green
6—Medium Green
7—Dark Green

Number Chart (for future years)

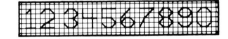

Seal and bow outlines and facial features—Black (backstitch with 1 strand floss)
Lettering—Dark Red (backstitch with 1 strand floss, except dot i with
French knot)
Snowflakes—Silver Metallic (backstitch over green cross-stitch)
Nose—Gray

143

Continued on page 144

ORNAMENTS: MAKE ONE, MAKE ALL (Continued)

LONG-STITCH CHRISTMAS TREES
Instructions are on page 55.

Long-Stitch Cluster Diagram

Work long stitches
in numerical order given.

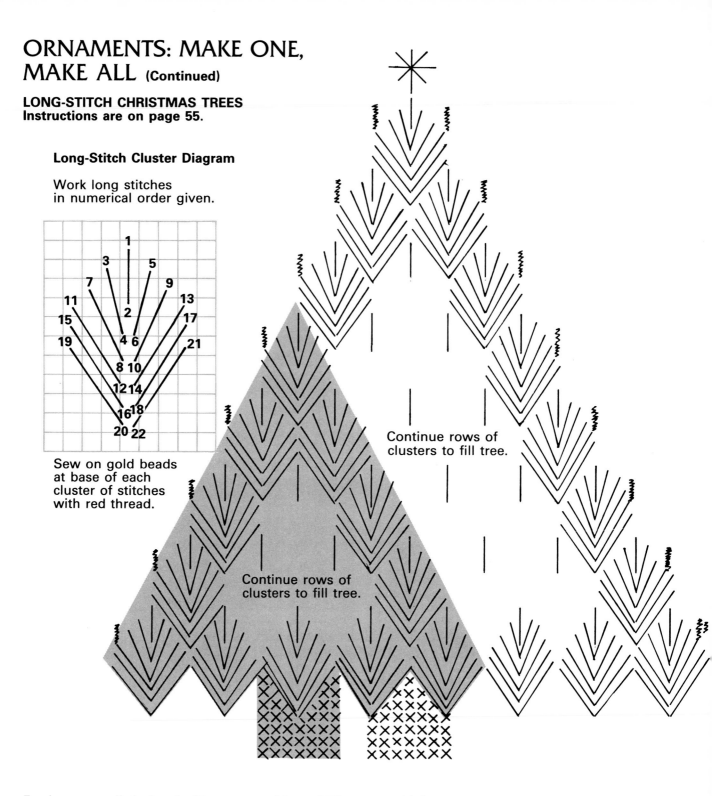

Sew on gold beads
at base of each
cluster of stitches
with red thread.

Continue rows of
clusters to fill tree.

Continue rows of
clusters to fill tree.

For box, overall design is 49 squares wide and 59 squares high.
For ornament, overall design is 31 squares wide and 41 squares high.

Shaded area is for ornament. For the box, work 3 more rows, adding 1 more cluster of stitches each time.
Reposition trunk for tree on box as shown. Add star to top of tree for ornament.

Color and Stitch Key
Tree—Green (long-stitch with 6 strands of floss)
Trunk—Brown (cross-stitch with 3 strands of floss)
Candles—Red (straight-stitch with 3 strands of floss)
Star—Gold (straight-stitch with 3 strands of floss)

PICTURE-PERFECT PADDED FRAMES
Instructions are on page 56.
Patterns are full-size.

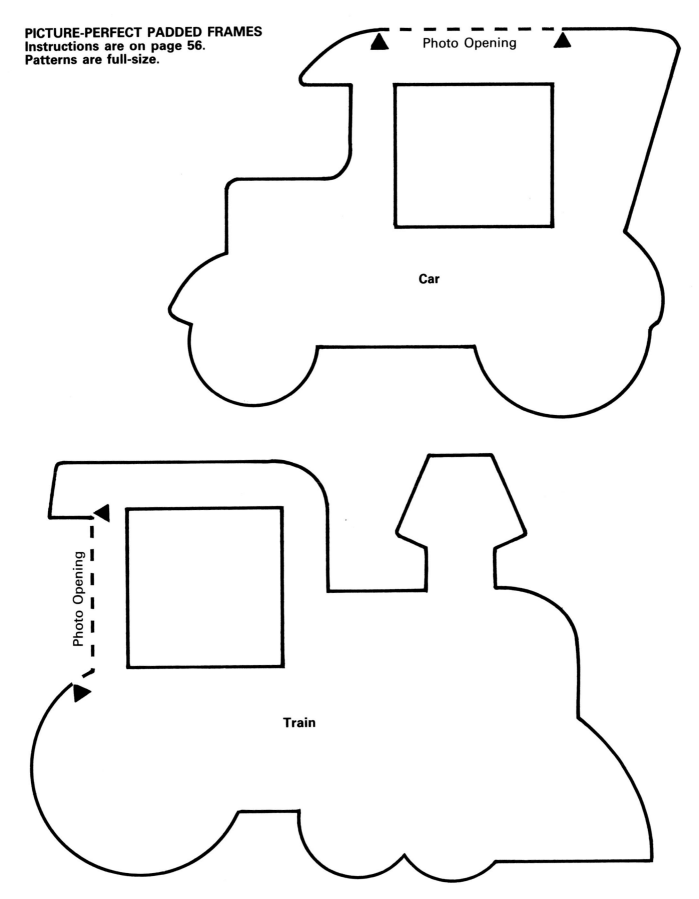

Photo Opening

Car

Photo Opening

Train

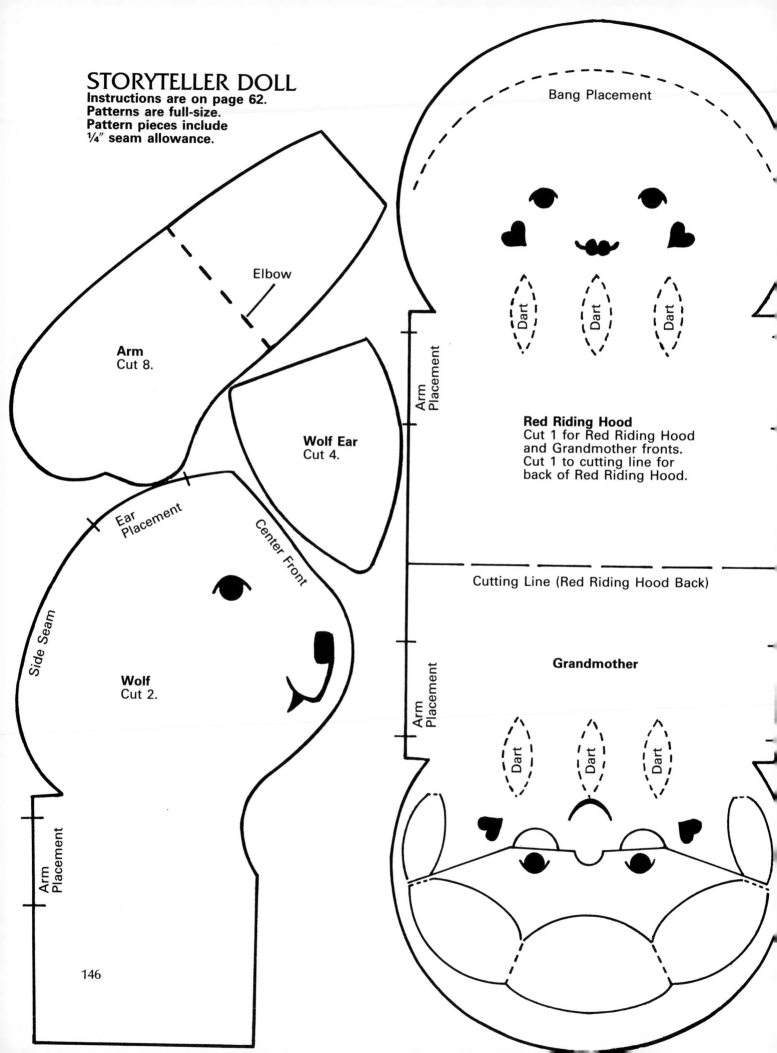

STORYTELLER DOLL
Instructions are on page 62.
Patterns are full-size.
Pattern pieces include
¼″ seam allowance.

Bang Placement

Elbow

Arm
Cut 8.

Arm Placement

Wolf Ear
Cut 4.

Dart

Dart

Dart

Red Riding Hood
Cut 1 for Red Riding Hood
and Grandmother fronts.
Cut 1 to cutting line for
back of Red Riding Hood.

Ear Placement

Center Front

Cutting Line (Red Riding Hood Back)

Side Seam

Wolf
Cut 2.

Grandmother

Arm Placement

Dart

Dart

Dart

Arm Placement

146

A CUDDLY PILLOW OF LOVABLE LAMBS

**Instructions are on page 60.
Patterns are full-size.**

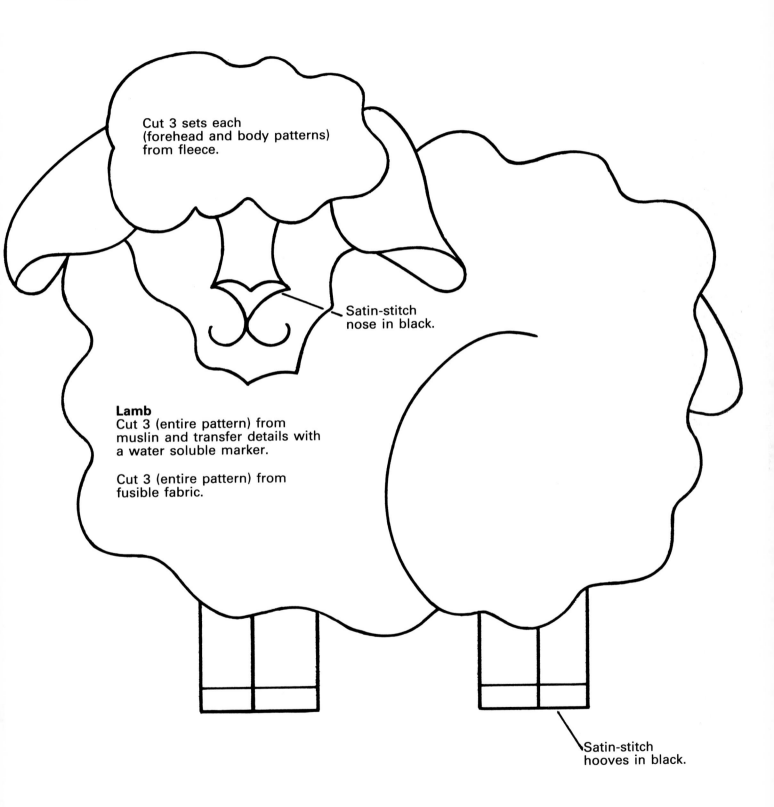

Cut 3 sets each
(forehead and body patterns)
from fleece.

Satin-stitch
nose in black.

Lamb
Cut 3 (entire pattern) from
muslin and transfer details with
a water soluble marker.

Cut 3 (entire pattern) from
fusible fabric.

Satin-stitch
hooves in black.

STENCIL, THEN QUILT, FOR PRETTY PILLOWS

Instructions are on page 84.
Patterns are full-size.

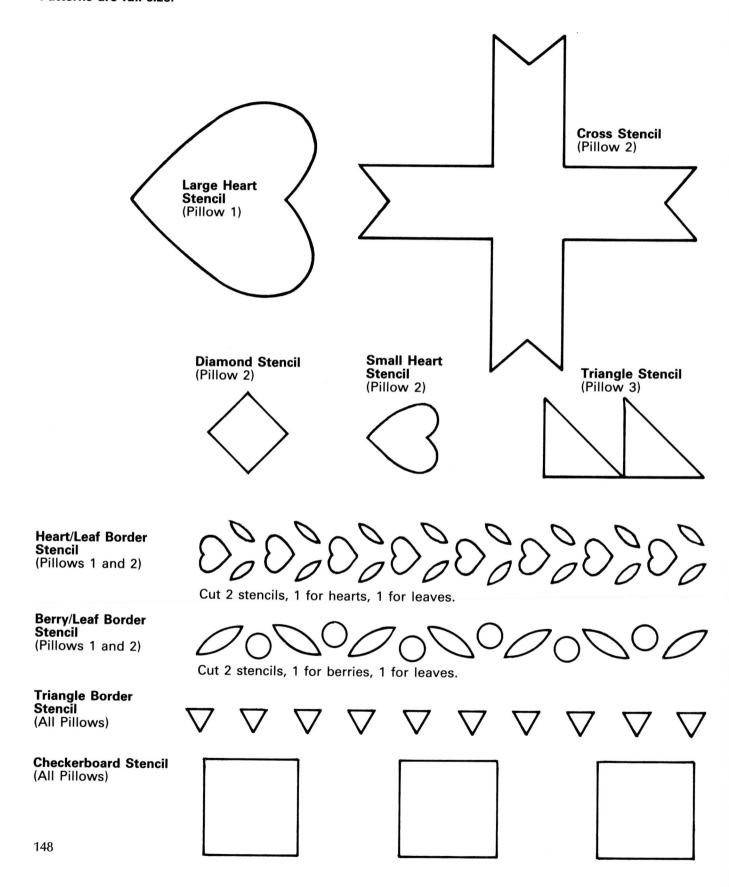

Cross Stencil
(Pillow 2)

Large Heart
Stencil
(Pillow 1)

Diamond Stencil
(Pillow 2)

Small Heart
Stencil
(Pillow 2)

Triangle Stencil
(Pillow 3)

Heart/Leaf Border
Stencil
(Pillows 1 and 2)

Cut 2 stencils, 1 for hearts, 1 for leaves.

Berry/Leaf Border
Stencil
(Pillows 1 and 2)

Cut 2 stencils, 1 for berries, 1 for leaves.

Triangle Border
Stencil
(All Pillows)

Checkerboard Stencil
(All Pillows)

148

FOLK-PAINTED HEARTS AND BEARS
Instructions are on page 73.
Patterns are full-size.

Large Heart

Painting Detail
(large heart)

Bear
Placement

½ of pattern.
Reverse for other half.

Bear and
Small Heart

Nail bear to
large heart here.

Painting Detail
(small heart)

149

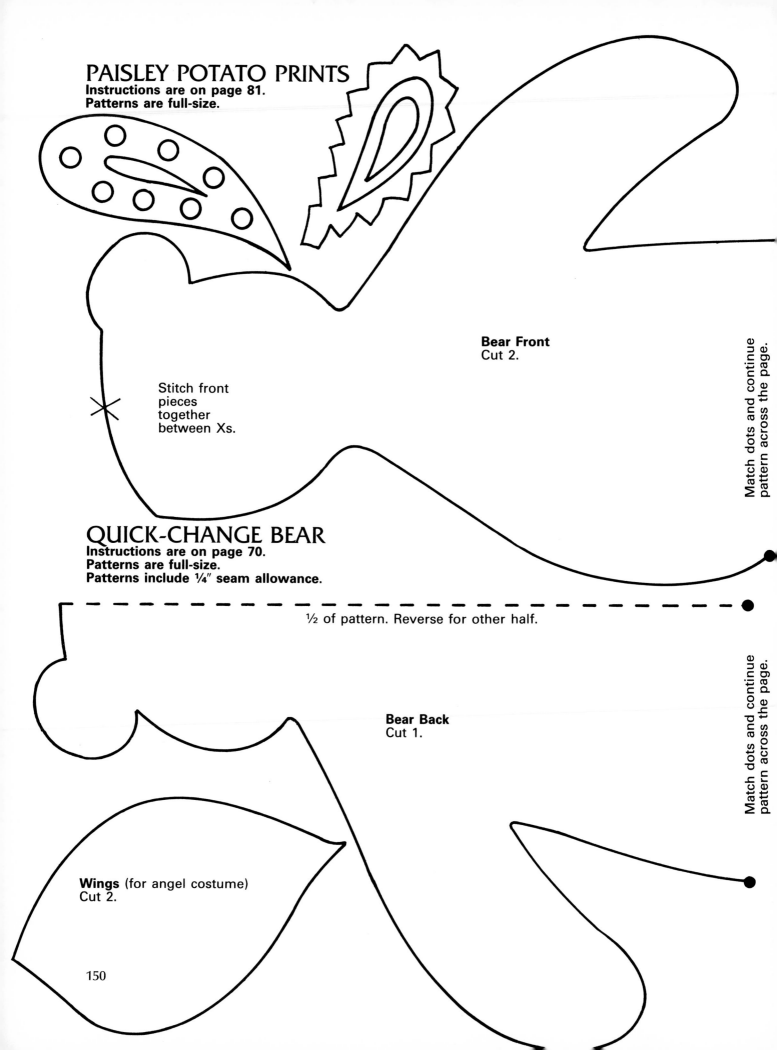

PAISLEY POTATO PRINTS
Instructions are on page 81.
Patterns are full-size.

Bear Front
Cut 2.

Stitch front
pieces
together
between Xs.

QUICK-CHANGE BEAR
Instructions are on page 70.
Patterns are full-size.
Patterns include ¼″ seam allowance.

½ of pattern. Reverse for other half.

Match dots and continue pattern across the page.

Bear Back
Cut 1.

Match dots and continue pattern across the page.

Wings (for angel costume)
Cut 2.

A FOLDER FULL OF GREETINGS

**Instructions are on page 82.
Patterns are full-size.**

Trace and cut stencil for A.

A....is for Apple

APPLE NOTE CARD FOLDER

Stem
Placement

Anchor ribbon
beneath apple.

Apple Appliqué

Match dots and continue
pattern across the page.

Stitch front pieces
together between Xs.

APPLE NOTE CARDS

Apple Stencil

Match dots and continue
pattern across the page.

Heart (for angel costume)
Cut 4.

151

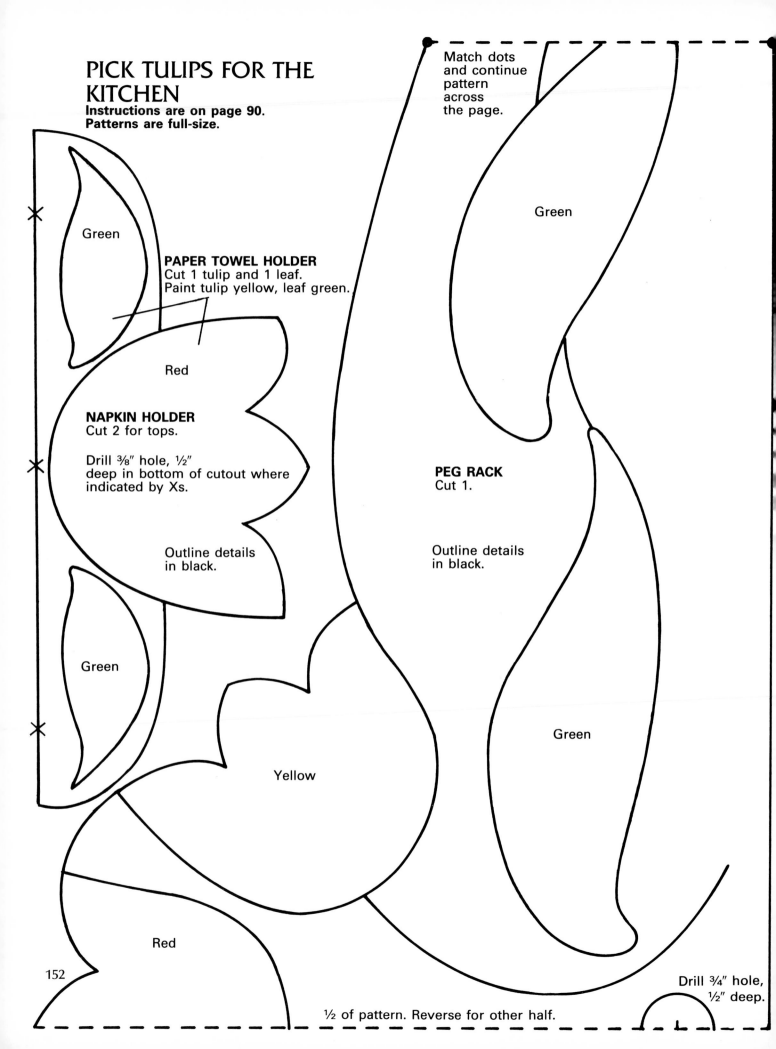

PICK TULIPS FOR THE KITCHEN
Instructions are on page 90.
Patterns are full-size.

Match dots and continue pattern across the page.

Green

Green

PAPER TOWEL HOLDER
Cut 1 tulip and 1 leaf.
Paint tulip yellow, leaf green.

Red

NAPKIN HOLDER
Cut 2 for tops.

Drill ⅜" hole, ½"
deep in bottom of cutout where
indicated by Xs.

PEG RACK
Cut 1.

Outline details
in black.

Outline details
in black.

Green

Green

Yellow

Red

½ of pattern. Reverse for other half.

Drill ¾" hole,
½" deep.

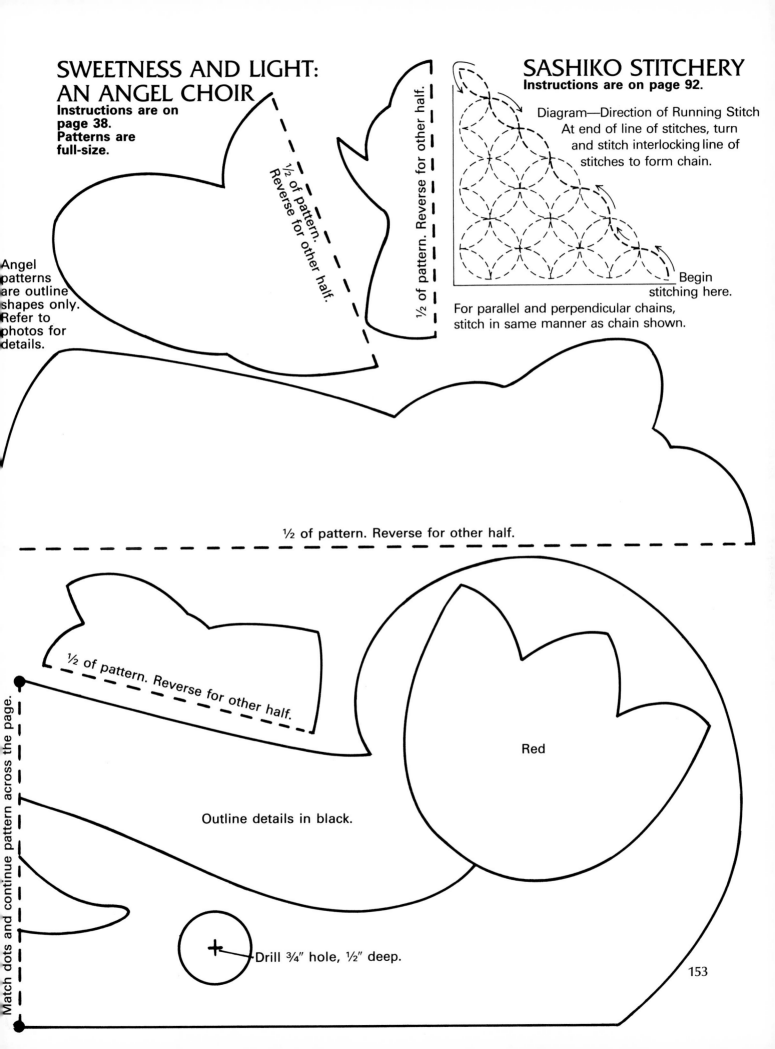

SWEETNESS AND LIGHT: AN ANGEL CHOIR
Instructions are on page 38. Patterns are full-size.

Angel patterns are outline shapes only. Refer to photos for details.

½ of pattern. Reverse for other half.

½ of pattern. Reverse for other half.

SASHIKO STITCHERY
Instructions are on page 92.

Diagram—Direction of Running Stitch
At end of line of stitches, turn and stitch interlocking line of stitches to form chain.

Begin stitching here.

For parallel and perpendicular chains, stitch in same manner as chain shown.

½ of pattern. Reverse for other half.

½ of pattern. Reverse for other half.

Match dots and continue pattern across the page.

Outline details in black.

Red

Drill ¾" hole, ½" deep.

153

CONTRIBUTORS

Carol Pladsen
Victorian Swan Tree Skirt........................ 24
Heart Potpourri Ornament....................... 26
Swan Ornament...................................... 27
Wreath Ornament................................... 28
Floral Cornucopia................................... 28
Fan Ornament... 28

Norma L. Richardson
Plastic Canvas Ho Ho Ho Ornament...... 55

Mimi Shimmin
Heart of Felt Ornament........................... 52
Paisley Potato-Print Sweatshirts................ 81

Kathleen A. Taylor
Mouse Angel Ornament........................... 46
Kitty Angel Ornament............................. 46
Teddy Bear with Costumes...................... 70
Stenciled and Quilted Pillows................ 84

Carol M. Tipton
Tabletop Dowel Tree.............................. 30
Wooden Panda Stocking Holder............. 36
Wooden Angel Mantel Decoration.......... 45
Crocheted Child's Vest........................... 66
Hankie Doll... 87
Tulip Paper Towel Holder....................... 90
Tulip Peg Rack....................................... 90
Tulip Napkin Holder............................... 91

The Vanessa-Ann Collection
Fabric-Covered Gift Boxes....................... 78

Volunteers Of North Carolina Botanical Gardens
Natural Materials Ornaments................... 18

Carol Wagner
Sashiko-Stitched Place Mat...................... 92

Bill Whisenant
Ribbon Arrangements.............................. 16

Carol A. Wise
Sock Angel Decoration............................ 42
Apple Folder and Note Cards.................. 82

PHOTOGRAPHERS

Jim Bathie
10, 11, 12, 13, 18, 19, 33, 35, 36, 43, 47, 48, 50, 51, 61, 66, 68, 69, 73, 78, 79, top 81, 84, 92, 94, 97, 99, 102, 103, 109, 111, 114, 119, 121, 125

Gary Clark
title page, 1, 8, 9, 14, 16, 17, 22, 30, 31, 38, 40, 45, 49, 52-57, 63, 76, 77, 83, 90, 91, 106

John O'Hagan
2, 4, 5, 6, 7

Courtland William Richards
cover, 21, 24, 25, 27, 29, 41, 42, 58, 62, 70, 71, 74, 75, 80, bottom 81, 87, 88, 89

Special thanks to the *Oxmoor House* Test Kitchens staff for preparing recipes.

CREATIVE IDEAS FOR LIVING™

THE Creative Lifestyle Magazine

12 issues, $13.95.*

YOU'RE

active in career, family and leisure time
energetic in your outlook
creative in your approach

GIFTS AND NEEDLECRAFTS

CREATIVE IDEAS FOR LIVING™ is for you!

CREATIVE IDEAS FOR LIVING™ is as individual as you are. The perfect guide to expanding a lifestyle that sparkles with freshness and vitality.

FOOD AND ENTERTAINING

FASHION

CREATIVE IDEAS FOR LIVING™ helps you live more beautifully—for less. Less time, less wasted energy, less complication.

DECORATING

The ideas of our editors and other creative women across the country show you how to develop and expand your own unique style in everything you do. The advice, instructions, and photographs are all geared to make you the most creative you can be!

To receive CREATIVE IDEAS FOR LIVING each month, simply write to:
CREATIVE IDEAS FOR LIVING
Box C-30 ● Birmingham, AL 35283

* Rate good in United States. Canada, U.S. Possessions, and Foreign: $16.00 per year.